"This book is an exceptional step-by-step guide any entrepreneur can learn from because Stacy does an awesome job covering the right lessons with the right detail. The end of each chapter includes "Sign Posts" to help you take action on critical points along your path. And Chapter Two, in my opinion, is were the rubber meets the road for any business owner—learning how to deal with self-doubt, negativity, self-sabotage, and then the lessons of how to define your priorities and giving yourself permission to fail. Outstanding!"

—**Stephen Woessner,** CEO of Predictive ROI and Host of the *Onward Nation* Podcast

"Stacy is one of the most brilliant entrepreneurs I know. Anyone who can turn backyard dance classes into a million dollar preforming arts company is somebody to learn from! Her advice is motivating, practical, applicable & best of all she makes everything so much fun! If you're struggling to start, maintain or grow your business—you won't want to miss this book!"

—**Molly Marie Keyser,** Host of *Venture Shorts* Podcast and Ventureshorts.com

"If you are an entrepreneur, stop what you are doing and go get this book! Stacy takes the stress out of running your own business and makes it fun. She guides you in self-realization to better equip you for your journey ahead. She will enlighten you on how to deal with money, clients and your reputation. Stacy's book is one that I refer to time and time again to inspire me to stay in the game and win!"

—**Casey DeStefano,** International Executive Producer and CEO of CaseyDeStefano.com and Host of *Women with Balls . . . in the Air* Podcast

"Whether you are thinking about starting a business or have run a business for years, you can learn from Stacy Tuschl's insights and experience. In *Is Your Business Worth Saving?* you will gain practical, easy-to-implement advice on how to improve your business and take it to the next level."

—**Greg Hammond,** CFP®, CPA - CEO of Hammond Iles Wealth Advisors and Author of *You Can Do More That Matters*

"If you are a passionate entrepreneur but have wondered whether or not you can really make a go of your ideas and dreams, this book is for you. Stacy cuts through the noise of small business advice to help you ask the most important questions and identify your next steps forward toward success. If "Is My Business Worth Saving?" is your question, Stacy will help you find the answer."

—**Misty Lown,** #1 Amazon Bestselling Author of *One Small Yes*

"Stacy's book *Is Your Business Worth Saving?* is a much needed companion for the everyday entrepreneur. We've all seen the scary statistics of small businesses failing within the first year, five years, and ten years. Stacy's book can truly help those break through to success and reach their goals. It is about keeping a journal, too, which I found delightful. But the perhaps most valuable aspect of it is its radiant optimism."

—**Afraa Zammam,** Author of the International Bestselling Book *The Successful Kid*

"Stacy Tuschl's step-by-step guide to building a profitable business is spot on. There's a lot of work involved in getting a solid business off the ground, and Stacy hits on all the elements. The examples she uses from her own business and life are a road map for other entrepreneurs. If you're struggling to figure out whether your business is worth saving, read this book."

—**Cheryl Tan,** Host of the *Standout* Podcast and CEO of CherylTanMedia.com

"Stacy's book is packed with innovative ideas for business owners at every level. I highly recommend this book for any entrepreneur who's looking to break out of their comfort zone and build their dream business. The tools, downloads, and quizzes in this book are great for getting crystal clear on your next step."

—**Jessica Rhodes,** Host of *Rhodes to Success* Podcast

Is Your Business Worth Saving?

Is Your

A STEP-BY-STEP GUIDE

Business

TO RESCUING YOUR BUSINESS

Worth

AND YOUR SANITY

Saving?

STACY TUSCHL

Published by:
Victory Books Publishing
10001 St. Martins Rd.
Franklin, WI 53132

For ordering information or special discounts for bulk purchases, please contact:

Victory Books Publishing
info@stacytuschl.com

Cover design and composition by Jennings Design, LLC.

ISBN 13: 978-0-9968104-0-1

Library of Congress Control Number: 2015951723

Printed in the United States of America.

10 9 8 7 6 5 4 3 2

I dedicate this book to you, the entrepreneur who looked at the title of this book and already knew the answer to that question was YES.

I know you have what it takes to make your business succeed.

I believe in you, and I hope you never give up.

CONTENTS

ACKNOWLEDGMENTS

So many people have contributed to this book, both directly and indirectly.

I want to first thank Darren Hardy for encouraging me to write a book. I had been trying to write one for years, and after attending your High Performance Forum, I came home on a mission to make it happen.

Thank you to my writing partner Amy Anderson for making my good book great. I could never have done this without you. Erica Jennings, my designer, thank you for making my vision for the book a beautiful reality.

Also, many thanks to Misty Lown for your guidance and mentorship. I am truly grateful to have met you. Your big dreams keep pushing and inspiring me to be a better businesswoman. And to Jim Jozwiak, thanks for our weekly chats and the constant inspiration and motivation you give me. I appreciate all that you do.

Big thanks to all of my entrepreneurial friends who inspired me to do this. I am forever grateful for your support.

I want to give a heartfelt thank you to all my staff at The Academy of Performing Arts. I am so grateful to have such an amazing staff. You are all great leaders. Thank you for always holding down the fort and making APA an amazing place for our students.

To my grandmother, who is still such a strong force in my life, and my grandfather, who was an ever-present reminder of my potential, thank you for being such positive role models and leading by example. Without you, I may not have realized entrepreneurship was an option for me. You have forever influenced my life.

Thank you to my mom and dad, who have supported me every step of the way in everything I do. I am sure there are many days when you wish I were a little less ambitious, but no matter what, you are always there to help me with whatever I need. And also thank you to my sisters Jamie and Rachel, who continue to go above and beyond for me in all the dreams I pursue. I am so grateful to be able to work with both of you.

I send my love and gratitude to my husband Kent, who had no idea what he was getting into when he met the twenty-year-old me. You have been along for this entire crazy ride, and I am so grateful for the support you have given me.

And finally, thank you to my my daughters Tanner and Teagan. You are my "why." In everything I do, I think of you girls first. I am so proud to be your mom.

INTRODUCTION

As an entrepreneur, you are a special breed. Determined, strategic, creative, and passionate—you are more than a business owner. You're an innovator, a leader, and a change-maker. You see the possibilities in any situation, the potential in people, and the prosperity at the end of every rainbow.

And if you're like the many entrepreneurs I work with on a daily basis, you're drowning in all that awesomeness.

Whether you're a solopreneur or the owner of a company employing hundreds of people, much of the stress and pressure—not to mention the work—falls on you. At various stages of entrepreneurship, every aspect of running your business falls to you. You're the bookkeeper, the marketing "expert," the sales force, the customer service depart-ment, the human resources representative, the operations manager, and the fall gal. The success or failure of your company, with all the resources and people attached to it, comes down to you.

If you're an entrepreneur at heart, then you're willing to take on this kind of responsibility. But that doesn't mean you always enjoy it—or know how to manage it.

I grew up in a family of entrepreneurs. Living in Oak Creek, Wisconsin, a suburb of Milwaukee, we spent many holidays together around a dinner table that turned into a conference room. While listening to my relatives discuss the latest business challenge and solution, I learned early in life that the way to take control of my time and my finances was to own a business. This entrepreneurial bent was so hardwired into my thinking that when I graduated from high school, I started a business without even knowing I'd done it.

I didn't see myself as a business owner.

Have you ever realized that you learned something from your parents, grandparents, or siblings without even realizing it while it was happening? That's what entrepreneurship was for me. My grandparents owned an excavation company, digging basements and working heavy machinery on construction sites. I sat at a dinner table full of people who worked a family business they had started from next to nothing and built into a thriving company. And I listened as they lived their entrepreneurial dreams.

No one ever pulled out a chart of the benefits of running your own business. My grandmother didn't sit me down while I was in middle school to go over the ins and outs of business accounting. My grandfather didn't explain that owning a business meant working odd hours and going to huge lengths to make sure the business thrived and the employees were paid. And my uncle didn't give me a formal talk on having a succession plan in place.

No, I just watched them live the lives of entrepreneurs, and from their stories, I learned what entrepreneurship really meant. I got an education at the dinner table. I learned how to address customer service issues, how to maximize relationships with vendors, and how to hire great employees. I listened in as they dealt with crises like economic slumps or equipment failures just before a big job.

The funny thing is, even after these firsthand lessons in entrepreneurship, I wanted to be a teacher. Despite all the examples I had seen and lived, and even though some might say I was hardwired for entrepreneurship thanks to my family background, I didn't see myself as a business owner. I did what many of us do: I went to college and hoped to graduate and get a good job.

HOW A HOBBY CAN BECOME A CAREER

I had taken gymnastics as a kid, and in high school, I enrolled in my first dance class. I was fifteen years old—a late start for a dancer—but I tried out and made the high school dance team. We were competitive, traveling to other schools and cities to dance our routines. We competed for trophies, titles, and bragging rights as the best in the state. I even went to dance camp and started teaching there when I was seventeen. I had discovered a passion for dance.

After I graduated from high school in 2002, I enrolled in the University of Wisconsin at Whitewater, a city about an hour from my house. I had attended dance camps there and loved the campus. I was going to major in education. It seemed like a simple, straightforward plan: go to college, earn a degree, and become a teacher.

Dancing was only a hobby, not a serious career.

In that last summer before college, I was a staff member of a dance camp. We staffers traveled over the summer, going from camp to camp on university and college campuses all over Wisconsin, Michigan, and Illinois. The students who attended these camps were in high school, but as we traveled, I heard that in other areas, middle school teams also had the chance to compete.

Middle schoolers in Oak Creek had nothing like this. Only the high school dancers could participate in recreational dance teams outside of school. That last summer before college, as I taught classes in the warm summer on the sprawling campus lawns, an idea occurred to me: I could do something like this for middle schoolers in my city.

Today, these kinds of traveling dance teams for kids in middle school, and even elementary school, are all over the place. But back in 2002, they were rare.

A month after I had my idea, I created flyers and hung them up at the local middle school to start my own group. Just like that, I had made a choice. I didn't give it much thought, really. To me, it was just something fun to do in my spare time.

I was just about to leave for college and move an hour away, and I remember my parents asking, "Why do you want to do this? Why are you moving away but then trying to start something here?" They have always been supportive of me, but they could see I was pulling myself in two different directions, and they were trying to help me figure out how to pick one path.

I assured them the dance team idea was just for fun. UW Whitewater didn't offer dance classes at the level I was hoping for, and I wanted to be more involved in dance in some way. I assured my parents they wouldn't need to pay for anything related to my dance group. I was going to charge a fee for each student, enough to cover the costs of competitions and costumes. In fact, I wasn't getting any money out of the deal, either. I was volunteering my time because I loved dance, and I saw this as an opportunity to share that love with the middle schoolers in my area. I wanted to help them enjoy the same competitive team experiences the older kids had.

I set up for my first class in my parents' backyard. With only one summer as a dance camp teacher under my belt, I expected to be bombarded with questions from the parents, but they were just excited for the opportunity—and the low cost. They also seemed excited for me. I was still so young that I think most of those parents saw me as a second child. They were so good to me, and I'm still friends with many of those people today.

For the next couple of months, I taught on Sundays in our backyard, and then I commuted back to UW Whitewater during the week.

Toward the end of October, Wisconsin got too cold for outdoor practice, so the mother of one my students found us a finished basement in her church that we could use for practices. I can't believe the church didn't charge us anything to use their space, but they knew I was volunteering my time to help the kids. Everybody was just so good to us.

The following April, when the weather warmed up, we moved practices back to my parents' backyard.

After three years of classes, that backyard was just a big square of dirt. The fact that my parents let me trash their yard is amazing to me.

Wisconsin has very few times of year when green grass thrives, but we never had any because my dancers ruined it every Sunday afternoon.

The classes became pretty popular. I taught the basics of dance, as well as some competitive jumps and other moves that the girls weren't learning in their school dance classes. We were dancing the routines the high schoolers used. I was preparing my group to be the best high school dance team possible. After they were trained, we started traveling to fairs and local competitions in Milwaukee and Chicago. As they improved, we went to Disney World, New York, and other large national events.

These girls had never competed outside school before, but they started placing in competitions right away. Only three or four middle school teams would compete with one another, and our team skills were above and beyond our competition's.

Meanwhile, I was very unhappy at college. Not only was I commuting home every weekend to teach dance rather than enjoy the college experience of parties and social events, but I was also unhappy with my degree plan. UW Whitewater is an excellent school, but it wasn't the right school for me. Looking back, I should have done better research and put more thought into my choice. In high school, I hadn't thought of dance as something I would do for a living. I loved the UW Whitewater campus, but the more I taught my own dance team, the more I realized that I needed dance to be a larger part of my life.

After my first semester, I transferred to UW Milwaukee, twenty minutes from my parents' house. I moved back home and continued to teach my dancers on the weekends. The next fall, I switched my major to business and pursued a degree in marketing. I wasn't sure what I would end up doing with my career, but at least I was closer to home.

I had no idea then that—with seventeen students dancing in the dirt of my parents' backyard—I had already begun my career.

WHEN YOU REACH A TURNING POINT

You know the moment you realize that the dream you've been working on, a little idea you had for some extra money, or a passion you pursued for free has become a real business? It's the moment when someone asks you what you do for a living and you say, "I own my own business." It's a turning point.

As my business grew over the next several years, first into a small rental space, then into our own custom dance studio, and recently into a second custom-built location in another city, I've faced many turning points. I look back on each of them now and realize that rather than threatening the business, these moments defined it.

I can't tell you how many times as an entrepreneur I've asked myself questions like, "Am I really capable of doing this? Should I really continue down this path? What if I'm in over my head? How will I know what to do next? Is this worth all the time, money, and effort I've been putting into it?"

Passion is the basis of all my business endeavors.

My passion alone wasn't enough to build a successful, million-dollar business out of a few students in my parents' backyard—after all, I wasn't even earning any profits from those classes. But passion is the basis of all my business endeavors, and it's the answer to many of my questions. In fact, it's the answer to the ultimate question we all ask at the beginning of our entrepreneurial journeys:

"Is my business worth starting?"

If it's your passion, your dream, your heart's calling, then most likely the answer is "Yes." It's worth pursuing, fighting for, and—eventually—worth saving. What I've found over the years, though, is that this "Yes" is just a starting point.

As a wife and a mother, I know firsthand that running a business as a woman is challenging in ways that many professional business coaches will never understand. I don't say this out of cockiness or bitterness. I just mean that women and mothers have unique challenges as business owners. Put a bunch of us in one room, and within a few minutes, you'll hear several of us talking about challenges—from our kids' schedules to our client schedules to working in a male-dominated industry.

Add these challenges to the common business obstacles that many entrepreneurs face—such as drowning under the weight of debt, being spread thin by mounting responsibilities, or starving for clients—and passion certainly won't be enough to save your business.

WHAT YOU'LL GET OUT OF THIS BOOK

If you're like me and have reached out for business advice at conferences or in professional organizations, you probably found the solutions you are shown may be great for some people and situations, but they aren't a one-size-fits-all answer to your unique challenges. You need tools, know-how, and action from someone who not only understands your personal and professional challenges, but also helps you tailor a plan that fits your specific business and life.

I will give you proven, tested, actionable strategies to determine whether your business is savable and, if so, how to save it and your sanity.

That's why I wrote this book. I can't give you the passion you need to be an entrepreneur. Either you come to the table with that or you don't. What I will give you are proven, tested, actionable strategies to determine whether your business is savable and, if so, how to save it and your sanity.

We're going to look at where you are—a realistic assessment of what's going right and what's going wrong. We'll examine how your personal habits, disciplines, and attitudes are affecting your company. We'll dive into detail about common stumbling blocks like finances, marketing, and professional relationships.

Finally, you'll get the Business Rescue Roadmap, which we'll tailor specifically for you. Armed with this plan for action, you'll be able to move forward and take the consistent steps necessary to transform your business—and your life. You'll have discovered what is working and what isn't, and you'll know how to fix it.

And because I am so passionate about helping other entrepreneurs live the life I have found in my own career as a business owner, you'll get exclusive bonus content that you can access on my website. You'll find templates, examples, and worksheets to help you uncover problems, assess situations, and forge a plan for success.

Ready for a reality check? Dive in anytime at StacyTuschl.com/Tools.

My most fervent wish is that you've opened this book with hope in your heart—hope for saving your future, your business, and your sanity—and that you'll close it with a plan to do just that.

Now let's get down to business.

SUPPLIES FOR THE JOURNEY

As we move forward together, I suggest you gather the following tools to maximize the effectiveness of this book and make the most of the exercises you'll find along the way:

- ⊙ A journal or notebook

- ⊙ A favorite pen

- ⊙ A glass of wine or a cup of tea

- ⊙ A positive attitude

CHAPTER ONE

I was sitting in a huge lecture class at the University of Wisconsin in Milwaukee. It was 2005, and I was a twenty-year-old junior. As a freshman, I had begun teaching dance classes and coaching a traveling dance team in my parents' backyard. Started from a whim and a few flyers at the local middle school, three years later, my fun "side project" had grown from seventeen students dancing at local fairs to more than one hundred kids entering national competitions.

That day in 2005, as hundreds of coeds around me took notes and listened to our professor lecture, I sat there with my journal, writing down the pros and cons of why I should do this dance gig as my real job. I kept thinking, "The end of my college career is coming—fast. What am I going to do?"

All those dancers were depending on me. Some of them had become like family. We were killing it at competitions, and I knew there were more students who could benefit from our program, but we had outgrown the backyard—not before trampling it to death, mind you—and I still wasn't even paying myself. I had to decide: was I going to jump in with both feet and run this thing like a real business—or not?

Is this business worth saving?

When I sat down with my editor to work on this book, I knew I wanted to write about that moment in every entrepreneur's life when we ask ourselves, "Is this business worth saving?" When we discussed this question, the first example I gave was that day in college when I was making my pros and cons list.

I was forced to make a choice between walking away from something I cared deeply about in favor of a more traditional post-college job hunt—or throwing everything I had into saving the dance team and taking it to the next level. Should I cut my losses and chalk up the three years of volunteerism as a great experience? Could I simply walk away from the hundreds of hours of blood, sweat, and tears I'd put into that endeavor? Or could I truly commit to win and invest even more time, energy, and money into turning this hobby into a real business?

Here's the thing: This moment happens over and over. It's not just one critical point in the life of your business—it's something you will continually go through. New challenges come up, life throws you for a loop, and the world changes. Your business has to change with it.

Since that decision point in college, my business has grown from a backyard hobby to a thriving company with multiple locations and over forty employees serving thousands of clients. I've become a real estate investor and have turned my experience with investing into a profitable family endeavor. And thanks to people who continually ask for my advice and input on their own businesses, I've become a coach who enjoys working with some of the most passionate, successful, and wonderful entrepreneurs in the country.

Over the years, if I had been afraid to act in the face of that daunting question—"Is my business worth saving?"—I would have denied myself, my family, and my clients the benefit of sharing my passion and all of the prosperity, fulfillment, and fun that has come from it.

So before we move forward, I want to make another thing very clear: You are also worth saving. Your commitment, passion, and hope have already driven you to seek answers to your business challenges, make enormous sacrifices, and give of yourself in countless ways. This speaks volumes about who you are as a person. Whether or not this particular business is successful, *you* are a success. You are worth the effort of going through this book, completing the exercises, and taking action to realize your dreams. Everyone has to start somewhere, and I'm honored to set out on this life-changing journey with you.

START WITH THE QUESTIONS

When I hit that first make-or-break moment three years into running my dance team hobby, I had no idea how far-reaching the consequences of my decision to commit to win would be.

I had so many unanswered questions . . .

⊙ Should I risk working this hobby as my real job?

⊙ Can I rely on it for an income?

⊙ Should I give up my free time, my money, and my post-college job hunt for this endeavor?

For an exercise to work through your own questions, visit StacyTuschl.com/ Tools.

⊙ Will anyone help me, or will I be able to do it all on my own?

⊙ Where will we meet now that we have outgrown the backyard?

⊙ How will I pay for that space? Should I buy or lease?

⊙ What kind of other expenses will I have, such as insurance, supplies, and payroll?

⊙ How will I get the word out to other potential students?

⊙ Am I crazy for thinking this could work?

In the end, I found answers to all of those questions, but it didn't happen overnight.

First, I listed my questions. Then I went through them one by one and developed a plan. The most important question to answer was whether I was going to do this thing wholeheartedly.

I think I had already known the answer to that one when I made that pros and cons list in class, but for months, I kept going back and forth with my decision. I think the more time I spent struggling through the answers to the other questions, the more I just knew the right thing for me was to start a business.

However, I had to answer those other questions before I could commit and take any action.

The choice to save—or start—a business begins with whether we have a passion for it. I loved dance and still do. I started teaching middle schoolers and taking them to competitions because I wanted to share my love of dance with others. It was a great way for me to be involved with dance while pursuing my business marketing degree in college, but I never intended it to be a full-fledged business.

Without that early passion as the seed, the business never would have blossomed, and I never would have found the courage, inner reserves, and commitment necessary to grow it over the years. But the passion alone wasn't enough to make a viable business.

In the end, I had to answer all of my questions to make a final decision about whether my business was worth saving. That's what you and I are going to do throughout the course of this book. We're going to uncover the questions you should be asking, and then I'll line you up with ideas and strategies to help you answer them.

TAKE A REALITY CHECK

Where are you in your business right now? Are you struggling, floundering, or doubting?

This is a big question: "Is this business worth saving?" I can't give you an easy answer. Anybody who tells you that passion alone will save your business is living in a dream world. Again, passion is a vital and foundational ingredient, but without additional ingredients like fiscal responsibility, marketing savvy, and hiring know-how, your passion will fizzle under the weight of a dying venture.

The trouble is that most of us don't want to look at the problems. I meet with entrepreneurs frequently who tell me that they don't even want to know how bad things are right now. They know they have a debt problem, but when I ask them how big their debt is, they say they don't know—and they don't want to know.

I get it. The kinds of problems that can kill a business are scary. They are confusing. And they often spring from our own insecurities, inadequacies, and lack of experience. Who wants to shine a light on any of those?

It can seem easier to leave bills unopened, avoid the conversations, and put busy work in front of the real work of saving your business.

But in the end, you are the one who suffers the most. When you allow fear to destroy your passion, you kill your dreams.

What would have happened if I'd sat in that classroom in 2005 and decided that the cons list was too scary to face? What if I had called all one hundred of my students and their families and told them I was shutting down the dance team? What if I had finished my business marketing degree and applied for corporate jobs like the rest of my classmates did?

The sky wouldn't have fallen, but by denying my passion, I would have sentenced myself to a life of mediocrity and unfulfilling days. I might have found a decent job with good pay and reasonable hours. I might have had nice coworkers and a short commute. But would I have been happy? I doubt it.

Because in my heart of hearts, I know I am supposed to be an entrepreneur.

Do you?

If the answer is yes, then it's not only time for a reality check, it's also time to pay up. Don't let the fear of what you have to do or say to make the necessary changes prevent you from being the person you know deep down inside that you can be. Don't let creditors, customers, friends, relatives, competition, the economy, or your own nagging voice stop you from pursuing your dream.

Have the guts to face
the music. It's the
only way you'll ever
be able to dance.

Have the guts to face the music. It's the only way you'll ever be able to dance.

LOOK AT THE BASICS

As business owners, we have more in common than not, I've found. We share the same fears, face the same hurdles, and ask the same questions. Sure, some of us are better at math than others are, but really, we're alike. So let's look at some common areas of struggle for most business owners.

As you read these, start thinking about what areas are holding you back and keeping your business from moving to the next level. Also, think about the one area you suspect will be the first to kill your business altogether. We'll come back to this one later.

The Woman in the Mirror

The well-being of your business is directly tied to your own well-being. Are you fulfilled by what you're doing? Are you an emotional wreck after each long day? Do you sacrifice your physical health for speed or productivity? How do your family members feel about your work schedule? Do you even see your family? What about a social life, a business support network, and a passion for what you're doing? It's time to look at how your beliefs, habits, and lack of priorities may be holding back your business.

Money Matters

Financial savvy isn't always easy, but it is teachable. Are you drowning in debt? Do you avoid looking at the numbers, or have you given them over to someone you don't trust? What are your tracking and budgeting methods? How are you evaluating your investments and expenses? What system do you have for fair compensation? Are you meeting your tax requirements? When money starts to feel like the enemy, it's important to get some perspective and create a financial fix so you can return to profitability.

Your Business Image

Whether you have a nonexistent marketing budget or an unlimited store of resources, how the world sees your business should be in line with your values and goals. Are you making the most of your marketing dollars? Do you have expert input on your marketing strategy, or are you winging it? Do you know the profile of your ideal customer? Does your competition's marketing make you feel inadequate? The person who controls your public image is you, so educate yourself on the basics of marketing, and learn how your company can benefit from simple tactics.

Business or Busyness

Most entrepreneurs go through a stage when the business is running them and not the other way around. Do you feel yourself constantly behind schedule? Are you completing tasks that you could pay someone else less to complete for you? Are you afraid to delegate because no one else can do the job as well as you can? Are you killing your potential for new clients because you're too busy servicing the existing ones? Is your email a never-ending stream of backlogged projects? Take the bull by the horns, as they say, and learn some productivity hacks that will give you back the reins.

People Skills

When it comes down to it, we are all in the people business. Are you treating your team in a way that creates loyalty, productivity, and job fulfillment? Do you know how to hire the right team members? Have you given your customers a reason to come back again and again, or do you have a great product but no customer loyalty? Are you creating strong vendor relationships? Do you know how to inspire your community? How you deal with people will make or break your business in the long run, so it's time to get the right folks on board to stay.

Each of these areas routinely causes problems for entrepreneurs. Rather than sticking your head in the sand and ignoring them one minute longer, let me help you look at what's holding you back. We all need help now and then. I could never have built the business I have today if it weren't for people who had built successful businesses before me and were willing to lead the way.

We all need help
now and then.

TAKE ACTION

At the end of my junior year in college, I made the final decision that I was going to open a dance studio and turn my hobby into a real business.

My grandparents had operated a successful excavation business for decades. My entire family was in on it, and I was able to apply many of the lessons I had learned during family-dinners-turned-business-meetings of my childhood. It's essential to have good advisors and people who believe in your vision. I was fortunate to have all of that built into my own family . . . and just a few blocks away.

I talked to my grandparents and my dad about how to incorporate. They gave me some advice and directed me to their CPA and attorney, who held my hand the rest of the way.

In August 2005, I leased a studio on a flat stretch of highway between Milwaukee and Racine County to the south. The space, surrounded by farmland and bordered by trees, had been vacant for about fifteen years. I had lived near there my entire life and could not remember a business ever inhabiting that building. When the property owner met me, I think he saw me, a young girl, and figured I wasn't going to make much money out of this endeavor, so he charged me only $1,500 rent for a large space that took up the entire right side of the building. I was bringing in $3,000 a month at that point in fees from my students, so I immediately said, "Yes, let's do it!"

I went to the hardware store and used all of my savings to buy flooring, mirrors, and ballet bars. Two weeks later, on August 21, my twenty-first birthday, we opened—as Studio 21. (Yes, I thought it was catchy at the time, but we've since changed it.)

By our second year in the rented space, my client list had grown, I had hired two teachers, and I was able to rent the left side of the building. Of course, my rent doubled. Although money was still tight, I knew I could afford the other side of the building once we pulled in new students to fill those new classrooms. I could see the potential, and it was exciting.

My little business had been saved, and so had my dream. I had crossed a major hurdle of my race. Now I had to figure out how to survive the inevitable next hurdles, when I'd have to decide, once again, "Is this business worth saving?"

SIGN POSTS

At the end of each chapter, I'm going to point out what I call Sign Posts. On any difficult journey, we all need a little reassurance that we're headed in the right direction. As we take this path together, pay attention to these Sign Posts, take action as needed, and then keep moving.

1. Ask yourself this question now: "Am I going to jump in with both feet and treat this like a real business?"

2. Don't allow fear to kill your dreams or destroy your passion. If you've come this far, you are a woman of courage and commitment. Now it's time to learn how to act on that courage.

3. Look around. Observe how far you've come since you originally got the idea for your business. Focusing too much on the road ahead can be intimidating. Take stock of where you are now, and write a gratitude list for all you've accomplished so far.

CHAPTER TWO

I f I asked you to make a list of all the things standing in the way of your business's being a huge success, you'd probably be able to open a blank page and start right away. "So-and-so isn't giving it her all, such-and-such price is too high, and this or that is keeping me from doing what I want," and so on.

It's natural to start looking at a problem from the outside in. I'm going to ask you to go against the grain and start by looking at the inside first.

Let's look at the woman in the mirror.

A business is an extension of the people who run it. As the business owner, you have the most significant impact on how your business is run and on the daily and long-term culture of that business.

How you act, what you say, and which beliefs and habits you bring to your business all shape how your business grows and expands—or shrinks and withers.

Most of the time, the business owner is the last to know about the immense impact her own behavior is having on her business. Your employees probably see it. Your vendors may see it. Even your customers may be aware of behaviors and beliefs that are keeping you from reaching your entrepreneurial potential.

Rather than take an embarrassing poll, let's walk through some common stumbling blocks for business owners.

SELF-DOUBT

Once I had incorporated my dance business, my family and friends really got on board. It was as if the act of calling it a real business helped them think of it as one. "Oh," they all said, "she's really doing this!"

You're not giving yourself enough credit.

Having an official studio space with our sign on the door certainly helped me see it as a real business too, but I still went through a weird transition of *knowing* it was a real business while learning how to *act* as if it were a real business.

I remember answering the phone, "Studio 21!" and fearing that the person on the other end was thinking, "Oh, how cute that she's pretending to run a business." Whether hiring two new employees or dealing with customer service issues, I had a nagging sense that I was just an amateur playing at a professional business game.

Every entrepreneur deals with self-doubt, but I think women in particular face a kind of inner negativity that needs to be addressed if we're going to succeed.

Female entrepreneurs are on the rise, but we're still outnumbered by men in many industries. When we put out a shingle and start calling our passion a real business, we often are harder on ourselves than anyone else is. We tell ourselves that people think we're frauds, fakes, amateurs, and worse.

Negative self-talk harms you—and those around you. I was at a seminar once, talking to a fellow attendee about a business challenge of mine. I said something about how I didn't feel I was capable of handling that particular issue. The woman looked at me and said, "You're not giving yourself enough credit. The people in this room all started somewhere. If you're talking so negatively about yourself, people will start to see that."

It had never occurred to me that others could see the effects of what I had been silently saying to myself. Remember that your employees, your family and friends, and your peers see you as an entrepreneur as soon as you believe you are one and start acting like it.

We've all heard those speakers who start their talks by saying, "I'm not really a great speaker, so bear with me." Why would you start a speech that I'm supposed to sit and listen to attentively for thirty minutes by telling me you're a terrible speaker? Now I'm *also* thinking you're a terrible speaker, and you haven't even started your speech yet!

It's unrealistic to think that we can be completely rid of self-doubt, but *sometimes* we can fake it until we make it. You can pretend you have confidence, speak well of yourself in front of others—or at least don't insult yourself—and go in there as if you know exactly what you're doing.

The more I *acted* as though I were running a real business, the more I felt like I was truly living the part. And it turns out that when you treat your business—even if it's a solo operation you run out of your spare bedroom—like it's a real business, the business grows.

The bigger we grew, the more clients we served. The more exposed we became in the community, the more at ease I felt. People would say, "I see how busy your parking lot is," or, "I saw you in the newspaper." Those comments started to make me feel that I was actually doing something big, something real, despite the lingering self-doubt.

In truth, I can't believe how much we actually grew in those first few years in the rental studio. I think about what would have happened had I treated this "hobby" like a real business from the start. I believe we would have had the same explosive growth. However, at that point, I didn't have the ability to think of it like a business yet, so no one else did either.

NEGATIVITY

Your own brain isn't the only place where you hear negative voices.

The world seems to be run on a 24-hour news feed these days. I have learned to avoid the news unless it's necessary. Most news outlets show the worst of our day rather than the best. I choose not to fill my head with that kind of thinking because how I think influences how I behave.

What we think about regularly affects how we see the world, our businesses, and ourselves. If I spend all day watching news reports about the failing economy, I'm likely to see my business as doomed, whether I'm turning a profit or not. That kind of attitude will seep into how I treat clients, how I forecast my financial outlook, and how I handle inventory.

I'm not saying that the economy has no effect on how we run our businesses, but the daily minutiae of the news doesn't help me run a more effective business—it makes me feel more afraid, angry, or hopeless. I can guarantee you that none of those negative emotions help you build a successful business.

Shutting off the TV or staying away from negative strangers is relatively easy in most cases. But there are situations where negative people can't be avoided. Then what?

Friends and family are often some of the most negative people, even if they don't mean to be. Sometimes when people know us well, they feel they can express their fears about our business decisions openly. This is all well and good until every time you see your friend or call your distant relative, you end the conversation feeling worried or defeated.

Women can be incredibly supportive of one another, but we also can be critical. As a female entrepreneur who also is a wife and mother, I have a different lifestyle. I'm not a stay-at-home mother who goes to playdates or the zoo. I'm not a working mother who passes the hours 9 to 5 at her office and comes home every evening like clockwork for family time. Most of the other moms I meet have a tough time relating to me—and me to them.

There are also certain societal expectations placed on me that can be hurtful or hard to manage. When I travel, outsiders may look at my family and say, "Oh, that poor child without her mother." They may question my work–life balance or my use of sitters to get my work done while still at home.

As female entrepreneurs, we are sometimes in a no-man's land, so to speak. We are unique, and when you're different from the average woman, that can arouse criticism.

If your friends aren't supportive of your business endeavors, or if they constantly raise doubts and fears about your professional life-style, try spending a little less time with them. I realize this is a sacrifice, but when you're running a business, you have to surround your-self with positive people who care enough to back up their good intentions with positive words. Not everyone can think big enough to do this.

Try to find friends who also are entrepreneurs. A local seminar or business networking organization is a great place to start. The women you meet at these events are more likely to empathize with your choices.

Family is trickier. Most of the time, I advise my clients to keep their answers about business short and to steer the conversation else-where. For example, when a notoriously negative cousin asks how your business is going, you can say it's going well, and then change the subject.

Surround yourself with positive people who care enough to back up their good intentions with positive words.

For those people who are in your inner circle—your parents, kids, spouse—this is a tough topic. It's natural for them to worry about you and want the best for you, but sometimes that concern comes out in the form of doubts and negative comments. You have the option to be straightforward with them: "When you say things like that, it makes me feel as though you don't support me."

Be prepared to answer their questions. Often, your loved ones are simply scared. Maybe they don't have the same adventurous spirit as you do, or perhaps they are more inclined to shy away from risks. Show them your financial projections, business plan, or marketing strategy to help them understand that you are going in with your eyes open.

If you don't feel you can have a hard conversation, or if you've tried and nothing has changed, you may need to avoid discussing that aspect of your life with a particular person. I have a friend who attends seminars and always leaves her husband at home because he is such a naysayer. It's sad, but she feels passionate about her business and doesn't want to let the negativity coming from her husband stand in her way.

The fact is that there will always be
people who doubt your ability to
build a successful business. If you
believe in your passion and your
abilities, then you may need to
push ahead on your own and seek
mentors and cheerleaders elsewhere.

Need help with your financial
projections, business
plan, and other basics?
Visit StacyTuschl.com/
Tools.

SELF-SABOTAGE

One of my favorite quotes is, "Don't be the smartest person in the
room."

When I started my business, I looked to my family for help. A lot. I'm
fortunate to have mentors built into my family, but whether or not
you know other entrepreneurs, you can get the same benefits.

But realize this: it's up to you to ask for help.

Too many entrepreneurs run their businesses with a chip on their
shoulder. They feel they need to have all the answers or find them on
their own. They don't ask for help from those who have gone ahead
of them and forged the way already.

Whether it's a professional organization, friend with a business, or
family member, seek help and be teachable. As soon as we shut ourselves off to input from others, either by ignoring their advice or by
not asking for it in the first place, we lose. And our business loses, too.

Learn to accept help. I like seeking out experienced people in my
industry at conferences and seminars. I also like talking with people
who are not in my industry so I can think outside the box. I want to

bring new ideas and approaches to my business that others in this industry aren't doing. Often, I get those new ideas from other entrepreneurs who have already proven they work.

Don't sabotage yourself by thinking you should or could do everything on your own.

I love books by John Maxwell, and one of the things he recommends in *Good Leaders Ask Great Questions* is the learning lunch. He suggests that you call someone, and ask if she is free for an hour to discuss some questions you have about her business. If she (or he) says yes, then prepare the questions. I've been doing this regularly since reading Maxwell's book, and it's been amazing. I have not been turned down yet by anybody I've asked.

Keep in mind that the last question Maxwell recommends that you ask your lunch partner is, "How can I add value to you?" Make the experience a give and take. You never know what you might have learned about or have the skills to do that could benefit someone else. This exchange of ideas is incredibly beneficial to your business, your reputation, and your self-esteem.

Here's a reality-check question to show you what I mean: Are your numbers getting better every year? If not, why not? Clearly, you need some input from someone else. Have you asked anyone? If so, whom?

Asking for help at all stages of your business is essential to its growth. As you move through the rest of this book and create your Business Rescue Roadmap in chapter 7, ask yourself who can best help you with each area.

The philosophy of asking for help and advice from others is the foundation of how I run my life. When I wanted to write a book, I started asking people, "Who can help me write a book? Who can help me create a website for it? Who are the big players that I need to call to make this happen?" I knew I wasn't going to do it all on my own.

If you're operating a one-woman shop—even if you think you're amazing—it's time to ask yourself where you need help. How can you get to the top in every area?

Self-doubt, negativity, fear—these stumbling blocks may be with you throughout the life of your business. It's human nature to be afraid, doubtful, and negative from time to time, but if you can watch for these things in yourself and take action to keep them at a minimum, you won't be the only one who benefits. Your business will reflect your improved attitude.

BUSINESS HEALTH STARTS WITH YOU

Let me tell you something that it took me several years to learn—I hope you can hear me and avoid taking as long to learn this on your own.

The health of your business is directly related to your own health. I'm talking about your physical, mental, emotional, and spiritual health. All of it affects the life and prosperity of your business—and everyone else involved with it.

So what happens when you've found yourself at a crossroads and are asking yourself, "Is my business worth saving?" Again, the first thing to do is look inward. How is your overall well-being affecting the well-being of your business?

Consider Passion

Are you passionate about this business?

Think back to the last period when times were tough—maybe that was yesterday or maybe it was a few years ago. Did you have a strong desire to push forward because you love what you're doing, why you're doing it, or the people you're doing it for?

That desire to push against challenges is an indicator of passion— and that's good news. Look, there are a lot of hard times ahead. That's the nature of owning a business. If you don't really love what you're doing, you won't be able to muster the stamina, strength, and courage you need to conquer those hard times.

But what if your answer to the above question is, "No," or "I'm just not sure anymore"?

In my industry, this happens all the time. A dance teacher is passionate about teaching. She loves her students, the performances, the music, and the sharing of her love of dance with others. She decides to open a studio. Two years later, she's miserable. She dreads going into the studio each day, and she wishes she could quit and get a regular day job. Why? Because she hates the day-to-day responsibilities of the business.

I was fortunate to learn that I loved the business side of running a studio as much as I loved the dancing side, but not everyone is like this.

Consider Strengths

Some people are "want-repreneurs." They love the idea of owning a business. They love the concepts of time flexibility and financial possibilities. However, when it comes to the nitty-gritty of running a business, they don't have the skills, the personality, or the willingness required to sustain a successful business.

If you've started a business and realized that entrepreneurship isn't your thing, the answer isn't always to shut down the business. My colleagues often bring in someone else to help run the operations side while they continue to teach dance classes and maintain a visionary role in the company.

If you feel as though you've lost your passion—or if you feel you never really had it to begin with—it's time to do some self-analysis. Think long and hard—not only about whether you love the industry you're in, but also about whether you're passionate about your role in that industry, its people, your customers, and the impact you're having on the world.

Not every business should be saved.

I know that's probably not what you want to hear, but the truth is that you don't want to waste your time and energy on something you don't love. As I said, your well-being has a direct impact on the well-being of your business. If you're not fulfilled, happy, and living your purpose, your business will suffer as you do. Why put yourself and everyone else through that when you could focus on something you truly love? Life is too short.

Did I lose you there? Are you throwing in the towel?

No? Great!

Let's get back to work. You have a business to save.

Avoid Tunnel Vision

Running a business takes time you didn't know you had. As a wife and a mother, I understand all too well that the idea of "balance" when it comes to time is a myth. The to-do list for every role in my life is simply endless, but this was true even when I was starting out.

By my junior year of college, I had been teaching dance classes (with no salary) for about three years in my parents' backyard and in a church basement. Despite our humble beginnings, my dance teams were rocking their competitions, and I had discovered a passion not only for dance but also for entrepreneurship. I decided to turn my hobby into a business.

My plan to incorporate was in motion, and I was looking for a studio space. I said to my dad, "I think I want to drop out of school. I really believe this business can work, and I think I can make money at it. Why do I need a degree that has nothing to do with dance?"

Up to that point, I had been fortunate that my parents were paying for my college education. My dad explained that he and my mother were far more than financially invested in my schooling. "You're a junior," he said. "You're graduating next year. You're going to finish. I don't care what degree you get, but you're getting a degree."

My parents actually both agreed with my assessment of the dance school. They told me they believed I could make a career out of it—they believed in my ability to succeed as an entrepreneur, and I'm so grateful for that.

But I'm also grateful that they pushed me to finish my education. Not only does a college education help broaden my perspective, open my mind to new ways of doing things, and teach me self-discipline and commitment, but finishing my degree also gave me a sense of accomplishment and self-esteem that I would have missed had I dropped out.

It also helped me refocus my thinking. I considered switching to a dance major, but what good would that do me when I was already running a dance school? I ended up earning a business marketing degree, which contributed immensely to my ability to succeed with my new company.

My parents pulled me out of a tunnel. I had been focusing so much on this dream of a dance school that I had begun to neglect my overall well-being. My singular focus might have kept me from achieving one of my earliest goals—graduating from college—and it would have denied me the benefits and lessons I learned from the (what I thought at the time was) "unrelated" degree plan.

Tunnel vision is a killer for entrepreneurs in so many ways. It alters our viewpoints, clouds our thinking, and pushes us to neglect our priorities and ourselves.

Define Your Priorities

Yes, we're all busy. We all have distractions, challenges, and conflicting obligations—but it isn't the conditions of your life that make the difference in how you spend your time. The issue isn't whether your plate is full. You're a woman. Your plate is full. End of story. Here's the issue: who do you want to be while you rise to those challenges, meet your obligations, and live out your priorities and values?

In the process of building a strong business, don't neglect your family. In the daily chores of being a great mom, don't sacrifice your physical health. Your pursuit of success in any one aspect of your life cannot come at the cost of the rest of what makes you who you are.

Lack of sleep while juggling every task at your business doesn't make you more productive. It makes you exhausted, grouchy, and less focused. Fast food every day for lunch because you feel like you need to be on call 24/7 doesn't make you a more effective leader, mother, wife, or friend. It compromises your body's ability to stay healthy and your brain's ability to make good choices. Skipping workouts not only weakens your immune system, forcing you to miss more days of work, but it also denies you important endorphins that push you to succeed and give you the enthusiasm to do so.

> Your pursuit of success in any one aspect of your life cannot come at the cost of the rest of what makes you who you are.

All of these unhealthy but common practices prevent you from setting a healthy example for your employees and your children.

They make you deny yourself the courtesies you would afford someone "more important." Would you treat your client to lunch at the drive thru? Would you tell your kids to skip a good night's sleep in favor of yet another item on their to-do list? Would you ask your spouse not to exercise in favor of helping you balance your books?

No. Why? Because these people are too important.

The question you need to be asking is, "Aren't I important, too?"

Let Yourself Fail

Remember the last time you failed? The really big failure when you questioned whether you knew what you were doing? Maybe other people questioned it as well. Scary, right?

I've had to tell people, "Yeah, I have this business, and it's not doing too well." Or, "Yeah, we tried this and it didn't go over too well so we're scrapping it." It's miserable. I hate the feeling of failure I have and the look of pity they have.

One year, I decided to bring music and acting classes to our school. We had changed our name from Studio 21 to The Academy of Performing Arts, and we were updating some of our offerings. I had a shiny, new vision of running a school that truly offered instruction in all of the performing arts. I was so excited about the music and acting classes—and I was sure the community would be as well.

But they weren't. Well, not for acting anyway. They loved the music classes, but we couldn't seem to get enrollment up for the acting classes. We did have a few wonderful students, and our acting coach possessed incredible talent. They worked hard and achieved good things together. Still, the community at large didn't seem to think of us as an acting school.

I talked it up among our existing clients, put out PR with every major media company we had partnerships with, and marketed the heck out of those acting classes. Still, they didn't bring in the kind of response that justified their expense.

So we scrapped them. It was heartbreaking for me. Not only because I had to give up my dream of a true performing arts school with all the offerings, but also because it was so public. By the time we took the classes off the schedule, everybody—and I mean everybody—knew we were offering them. I had done such a great job of getting the word out that when we canceled the classes, everybody noticed. And they all asked about it.

If you're not failing, you're playing it too safe.

There's nothing worse than failing . . . except failing publicly and having the same public conversation every single day about why you failed. Our clients asked what happened, my friends and family asked, strangers in line at the grocery store asked.

Failure stings even more so when others see it. But let me tell you this: as a business owner, you are going to fail, and you are going to fail in public. Get used to it.

If you're not failing, you're playing it too safe. You're not taking risks, and you're not trying new angles, approaches, and products. You're not working as hard as everyone else is in this entrepreneurial game.

So number one: Go out there and fail. Fail big if you need to, but don't be afraid to fail.

And number two: When you do fail, cry about it, eat some chocolate, and then let it go. Don't be someone who holds onto her failures. Those past "mistakes" are lessons you had to learn to become the woman and the entrepreneur you are today. If you're spending any part of your day beating yourself up about those, you're wasting time. And you're harming yourself—emotionally, physically, and financially—more than you realize.

Someone who is always conscious of her last failure walks and talks and acts like a failure. That's not who you are. So yes, fail. Then move on. Because the next risk you take just might be a success.

SIGN POSTS

In this chapter, we talked a lot about how your business is an extension of you—your thoughts, actions, and beliefs. Rather than being discouraged by this, be encouraged. This is good news. If you are the source of most of your business challenges, then the power to change them lies within you, too.

Your behavior is largely a product of your thinking. Negative thinking will stunt your ability to create new habits and be consistent. Start changing those old tapes in your head now by learning more about my exclusive program Focused Formula Bootcamp. This live event and online course will help you change your old tapes and your old habits. Learn more at www.FocusedFormulaBootcamp.com.

Assess your health. If you're sacrificing essentials like sleep, nutrition, and exercise in favor of business tasks, you're working against yourself. Are you willing to make even one small change today?

Write in your journal about the last time you failed big. Then write out the lessons you learned from that failure and how they've helped you. Putting a positive spin on mistakes will save you from bitterness and focus you on success.

CHAPTER THREE

We all bring our financial backgrounds to our businesses. Some of us grew up with good financial examples and others didn't. Some of us are savers, some are spenders, and some just get confused by the whole numbers game.

I assure you—no matter what your background is or what your perceived shortcomings are when it comes to managing money—that you can learn to create a strong financial future for your business.

I was fortunate to grow up in a house with parents who were financially savvy. Early in my life, they taught me the principles laid out by Suze Orman and Dave Ramsey. I'm a saver, and I always have been.

But that doesn't mean I don't have my own financial challenges.

Back in 2005, when I started teaching dance in my parents' backyard, I charged a fee from each student to cover competition entries and costumes. We weren't renting a studio space—even in winter, we used a donated space in a local church basement—so we had no overhead. I was the one doing everything, so I didn't have employees to pay, but I wasn't paying myself either.

I volunteered all my time. I loved dance, and I loved sharing it with those girls and their families. It was fun for me. Yes, there was some work involved, but it was work I felt passionate about. In fact, the more I worked, the better I liked it because I became closer with the families. I was only eighteen, and the parents of my students were very encouraging to me.

After about a year, one parent came to me and said, "Stacy, you really need to be charging for this." I thanked her but shrugged it off.

Then another parent came to me and said the same thing. She told me that I was providing a service, and they ought to be paying me. Other dance studios in the area charged reasonable fees that covered the cost of a teacher's salary. My students' parents pointed out that I was providing opportunities that these studios weren't offering. I was creating a unique and valuable service. Why shouldn't I be compensated for that?

I will forever be grateful to those parents. They helped me see myself as a professional. In a sense, they built my business for me. While I didn't take a salary for myself at the time, I did take more money for the lessons and turned that increase into a business savings account. Those parents were turning me from a volunteer into an entrepreneur, even if I didn't see it yet.

Whether your money problems stem from how you see money or from how you see yourself, they can kill your business. From looming debt to tax issues to improper goal setting, financial difficulties are often the primary reason you're asking, "Is this business worth saving?" It's time to educate yourself on which financial challenges are pushing your business to the brink and how you can overcome them.

GET PROFESSIONAL HELP FROM THE START

When I finally incorporated my business, my parents advised me to hire a certified public accountant, or CPA. They were right to point me immediately in this direction. (It's also the first thing I recommend in the financial section of the Business Rescue Roadmap.) They had worked with one person for years in our family business, and they suggested I meet with him.

For the first few months, things went well. At the same time I was asking for his professional help, I was also seeking more knowledge on my own. I educated myself on financial principles and tax requirements by reading books and blogs (I recommend you start with Tom Wheelwright's excellent tax tips).

One day, I asked my CPA a question about a financial strategy I had discovered. I realized that he was doing a good job with the tasks at hand, but he wasn't strategizing on my behalf. That might work well for someone with her own investment or tax knowledge, but it left me handicapped. I needed someone who could help me plan ahead, not just meet requirements.

I worked with the CPA for a while longer, largely because I was afraid to fire someone who had worked with my family's other business for thirty years. I put it off for a few weeks, hoping that there was a way around it. But in the end, I told this CPA—and my family—that I was going to hire someone else.

Today, I have a CPA who is qualified to guide me in the financial strategies I want to implement for my business, as well as in the tax requirements that are necessary. He has saved me a ton of money. In my first year, my taxes dropped dramatically, and I've continued to save money with his expert help.

When looking for a qualified CPA, look for someone who has certification and some experience in your industry, and who can also bring new strategies to your attention.

Ask around for referrals, but keep in mind that just because your family and friends use this person, that doesn't mean he or she is the right fit for you and your business.

I recommend allowing your new CPA to review your taxes from the year before and suggest how the previous year could be amended to save you money. Not only will this show you the difference between the new and old tax advisor's methodologies, but it will also save you some money that you can use toward hiring that new CPA.

Some firms charge by the hour, but I prefer to work with a CPA who charges a flat fee. If I have questions by email or phone, I'm not charged extra for that time. I often visit my CPA in person, and I have not been charged.

The most important factor for me is that my CPA is working proactively to maximize my income. I'm not paying someone to answer questions. I'm paying someone to raise questions. He contacted me a couple of months ago and said he pulled a report and he now recommends that I start taking more taxes out of my paycheck so I don't get hit with a big debt at the end of the year. That kind of strategic thinking and action—without my prompting—is one of the things I suggest you look for in your own professional partnership.

Pay attention to what's happening with your finances at all times.

Now, don't "set it and forget it" when it comes to money. You'll want a professional to advise you and guide you, and you probably want that same professional to prepare your taxes, your payroll, and a few other financial documents essential to your business—but pay attention to what's happening with your finances at all times. Let me tell you what can happen if you don't.

LEARN FROM OTHERS' EXPERIENCES

A friend of mine is a business owner. Let's call her Jane. Jane hired a family friend to manage her accounts. She gave him carte blanche to write checks on her behalf, fulfill financial obligations, pay bills, and keep all of her records, including profit and loss (P&L) statements. Each week, he would fill out checks with the recipient's name and the amount of the check. Then he'd present them to Jane to sign.

Well, it turned out he was filling out those checks with erasable ink. After she signed, he was altering the checks and cashing them. Sadly, Jane wasn't reconciling her checking account.

At some point, she noticed that her account balances didn't match the numbers she had in her head. She asked someone else to go back through her accounts and reconcile the previous months. What she found horrified her.

This person had cheated her, and he had done it while remaining friends with her family. Jane took him to court, and he was charged with embezzling more than $10,000 from her business.

She told me later that she never would have suspected him because he had been associated with her family for years, and she considered him a good friend. Unfortunately, when things get tough, people get desperate. Friendship isn't always enough to keep people honest.

Another friend of mine, we'll call her Carrie, hired an accounting firm to pay her business taxes. Carrie sent the firm regular checks to keep up with her various requirements. One day, she got a letter from the IRS stating that it hadn't received her latest form. She called the accounting firm and was told that the form had just been mailed, so the form and the IRS letter must have crossed paths. The firm assured her that she shouldn't worry.

Then Carrie received another letter. And another. This third one was much scarier. She made some calls and finally confirmed that the accounting firm had not paid a single cent of her tax debt. They hadn't filed her forms or communicated with the IRS on her behalf at all.

Now Carrie owed her original taxes plus penalties and interest as well—and she was out the fees she had paid to that accounting firm, which, by the way, had a good reputation.

The lesson here isn't that you can't trust anyone. It's that—no matter who's helping you—in the end, you are responsible for your money.

I never let a month go by without reviewing my P&L statements, my account balances, and other pertinent numbers. I strongly suggest you do the same. It's a few extra minutes on your to-do list, but it could save you a great deal more than that half hour if someone who's helping you decides to help himself or herself instead.

Debt is the most destructive financial challenge I see among business owners.

STOP THE CREDIT SPIRAL

Debt, by far, is the most destructive financial challenge I see among business owners. If you keep borrowing and spending—without paying it back—you are flushing your money and your business down the toilet.

Yes, that sounds harsh, but I want you to feel the full impact of how dangerous this debt habit is. And it *is* a habit. Most people with a debt problem don't have that problem because they borrowed money for one big-ticket item. They are in massive debt because they've spent months, years, even decades using credit to buy a lifestyle and a business that they couldn't afford. Over and over, they made the choice to spend money they didn't have on products, services, and resources they couldn't support without borrowing even more money.

Face the fact that you're in debt and that the debt is eating your business alive. Look at the bills. Add up the amounts. Get a realistic picture of how much you already owe to creditors.

Once you have a clear picture in your mind, analyze your debt. You'll probably find one of two scenarios here.

The first is that you think you're in so much debt that you may lose your business. Unfortunately, there is a point at which debt is so large that an entrepreneur may not be able to bail herself out and save her business at the same time. I caution you, however, not to make this fatal call on your own.

Don't stare at the lump sum of debt and think, "I'm never going to pay this off. I should just throw in the towel." A qualified CPA can guide you through a debt crisis like no one else can. Consult a professional financial advisor who will help you create a strategy to pay down your debt—and hopefully save your business in the process.

The second scenario is the most common: You're in a lot of debt, but not so much that it would ruin you. However, you aren't in any hurry to pay it all off either.

You're in this category if you're saying, "Yeah, but Stacy, I pay the minimum every month!" I have bad news for you: Paying a monthly minimum, while continuing to increase your debt on another account sends you spiraling deeper down. You are not digging your way out. You are digging a deeper hole.

I was raised to use credit cards to build my credit rating, not to afford a lifestyle beyond my means. I know this seems like a lofty goal to many people, but start small. If you've been paying the minimum, pay more. Again, get some advice from a professional on the best course for paying down your debt in a reasonable time.

I'm not saying it's bad to take a line of credit now and then. We all have off-seasons or crises that force us to borrow money until we can get back on our feet—but you must have a plan for paying down that debt or else you shouldn't take the loan.

To help you with this process, I highly recommend Dave Ramsey's Financial Peace University, a nine-week course you can take online or in person. My husband and I took it online the first year we were married, and hearing others talk about the same issues we were facing was helpful. I'm not exaggerating when I say that it changed my life. I recommend taking it with your spouse or your business partner, if possible.

I have a friend who has been struggling with debt for a while now. For years, I've told her about Dave Ramsey. Well, she finally took the course, and now she can't stop bragging about how much she has paid off and how much her savings has increased. She texts me every time she pays off a credit card. Her confidence is through the roof. In fact, she is now making her three college-age kids take the same course.

The goal should be to live within your means, save a little each month, and use credit only for emergencies.

The goal should be to live within your means, save a little each month, and use credit only for emergencies or to rack up airline miles. Pay off your balances monthly. If you have trouble doing this on your own, it's time to get help.

BUILD SUFFICIENT SAVINGS

So let's talk savings. Actually, let's talk expensive purses. And vacations. And cars. How many times have you seen a business owner driving around in an expensive car, only to learn later that her business is going bankrupt?

Yes, that's related to credit, but it's also largely related to savings.

A savings plan is not just a good idea; it's a crucial aspect of business ownership. If something happens that interferes with your ability to make a profit, that savings plan will literally save your business.

Look at your possessions, your lifestyle, and your habits. Are you sacrificing your savings for the latest handbag? Are you dipping into your business savings and paying yourself a bonus so you can take a trip to the beach? Is your savings balance lower than what you owe on your car?

I'm not trying to make you feel bad, and I'm not judging. I get it. We all like nice things. We love time away with our families. Many of us start businesses so we can enjoy time and financial freedom. But they come at a cost.

That cost is self-discipline; it's having the self-control to put money aside every month and not touch it unless it's truly necessary. Having a line of credit for a backup plan is fine, but your liquid savings balance is crucial.

Suze Orman says you need at least eight months of living expenses in an emergency fund. Dave Ramsey says three to six months is good. I lean toward the higher end because I like knowing I have that security. The confidence that comes from being financially secure allows you to make better choices than the desperate decisions you make when you're secretly struggling.

When you're just starting out, building an emergency fund can be tough. Keep at it. Little deposits add up over time. You are cultivating a habit of saving—and not touching—that money.

To help boost your savings, evaluate what you're spending. Are you investing your money toward the growth of your business, or are you only spending money?

Look at what things really cost, and you might find some hidden areas from which you can pull savings money.

Let's say I want to offer cable television in my lobby, so I spend a $100 per month on that service. I could offer Netflix instead at $8 a month . . . or I could get rid of it completely and offer only network TV stations. The questions I need to ask are, "What's the return on my investment?" "What's a necessity, and what's something extra that I could put off until I have more money?" "What's this perk for my clients really worth?"

Another example of this I see all the time is a website. If you don't have a brick-and mortar presence for your business, you may want to invest more in your website to make sure it's a professional, quality representation of your company. This isn't an area to skimp on, but you might hold off on the extra web pages until you're pulling in more revenue. These days, social media is a great substitute that might even result in more sales than a website will, depending on your industry and your following.

In the meantime, divert these funds to your savings. Again, the confidence you'll gain when you have a fully funded savings plan will surprise you. You'll feel empowered to make sound financial choices that are investments in your business rather than last-ditch efforts to bail yourself out of trouble.

LEARN MONEY MANAGEMENT

When I started my business, I was not an entrepreneur in any sense other than emotionally. I had a great passion for dance and for sharing it with others. As I experienced the thrill of a startup and the excitement of creating my own vision, I also developed a passion for entrepreneurship. Unfortunately, that didn't mean I immediately gained entrepreneurial skills.

Money management is one of the most important skills you need as an entrepreneur, but I've found it's often the one we lack. Most of us don't go into business ownership with a lot of knowledge of P&L statements, investing, budgeting, and other money management topics.

At times like these, when you're facing a turning point in the life of your business, the ability to read a P&L statement is more important than ever.

Your ability to manage your money will make or break your business. It may already have threatened to break it. Your inability—or unwillingness—to budget may be part of the reason you're in this mess to begin with. Or maybe your lack of oversight when it comes to your money has landed you in a deep hole you didn't know existed until it was too late.

Let me review the few essentials I use in managing my money effectively. Don't worry about following every detail of this right now. Just start getting familiar with these terms. We'll address what you need to do first when we get to the Business Rescue Roadmap in chapter 7.

The earlier you can establish these behaviors as habits, the better your financial outlook will be.

Reports

I needed a few years to learn this stuff. I wish I had gotten on board with these habits at the very start of my business, but, as they say, better late than never. The earlier you can establish these behaviors as habits, the better your financial outlook will be.

Eventually, I sat down with my excellent CPA and asked him what reports I needed to be pulling, what numbers I needed to be watching, and how often I should be performing these activities.

Before I let you in on what he said, let me just say that despite his excellent explanations, I stayed confused for a while. This is heady stuff for many of us. I'm no financial expert, and in the first few years of my business, I was struggling just to understand these practices, let alone stick to them.

This financial language is foreign to a lot of us, but don't let it hold you back. Work to understand it, apply it, and make it perform for your business.

The more comfortable I got with spreadsheets and reports, the more I came to realize that I got joy out of doing them. Not because I'm some huge spreadsheet fan, but because the clarity, security, and vision they gave me was priceless—and certainly worth the years of effort it took to master them.

My CPA told me there were two primary reports I should be running monthly. First, a P&L statement would show how much money was coming in and how much was going out—and in what ways. My P&L shows our tuition payments, fees paid to us, and any other income listed by type. Then it shows the payments we make to vendors, our payroll amounts, and any overhead we are charged monthly. Once we subtract the expenses (the loss) from the income (the revenue), we get the profit total.

Download sample reports and get more instruction at StacyTuschl.com/Tools.

I keep a close eye on this report. I know about how much we bring in each month, so if this report is significantly lower or higher than I expect, I take the time to search for the reason. It could be an error, so I make sure to find the source of any variation.

When you're first starting out, you won't have an average monthly income, but if you've been in business for a while, this is a number you should know offhand.

You still with me? Good. Just one more major report to review.

Next, my CPA told me to think of the second report—a balance sheet—as a report covering specific period. When I pull this report, I run it for a specific time frame. Maybe it's the first quarter, the month of January, or the first week of June. A balance sheet shows me a snapshot of the big number over any period. My CPA says this report should be run quarterly.

After he explained all this to me, I bought a $1 spiral notebook at Walgreens to keep my books in. Yes, I used a kid's spiral notebook to run my business books, and it worked fine for a while (although one day I thought I lost it and just about had a heart attack). The point is that you don't have to overcomplicate this aspect of your business. If you're comfortable jotting notes on paper, do it. If you need a calculator to add 2+2, fine. No one else cares. The important thing is that you make a start.

Today, I use QuickBooks online and can run these balance sheets myself any time I want to check the numbers. I can also ask my CPA to run this for me regularly—and if all of this still sounds confusing to you, you can do the same. Learn how to read your reports so you can catch any errors. It will get easier after a while.

Visit StacyTuschl.com/ Tools for easy access to tracking resources.

Here's the bonus: You can compare your numbers to the same period in the previous year. You'll get to see how you're measuring up to your goals. (No financial goals yet? Keep reading.) Check your expenses—are they increasing? If so, why? Look at your sales—are they flat even though you've brought in new clients?

One of the biggest breakthrough moments for me was when I realized that, many times, the spreadsheets brought good news.

We had more clients or took in more tuition than we did during the same period the year before. Why wouldn't I want to look at that?

The biggest red flag is raised when you are spending more than you're bringing in. That's a challenge, but it's an even bigger challenge if you don't know it's happening. These reports keep you current and aware of what's going on in your business so you can head problems off at the pass.

Budgets

None of these reports will do you much good if you don't have a budget—and use it. You can have a consistent income over several months yet show a different monthly profit because you aren't controlling your spending.

My business is seasonal. We tend to attract clients with the school year, so that's September through June. The problem I ran into early was that I kept spending in July and August as if we had the same amount of business as we did during the rest of the year. All of a sudden, I'd enter September and realize I was broke. I actually applied for a line of credit to hold me over more than once before I learned to use my budgets to keep my spending in check.

I also see this scenario often: A business owner starts doing well financially, and she decides she can suddenly afford the leather lobby chairs or the more expensive shipping containers. Then she spends the money and forgets that she had a property tax bill due the following month.

If you're not setting a budget, looking seriously at what you need coming in, and verifying what's going out each month, you're digging the financial hole again.

Every January, we start looking at our budget for the year. Again, I use QuickBooks for this process, and I monitor our progress monthly on the budget.

Sometimes, just seeing the budget in writing will keep you from overdoing it.

How do you establish a budget if you don't already have one? If you've been in business for a year or more, create a budget based on the numbers from last year. How much did you spend each month on repetitive services? How much did you spend on quarterly needs? Taxes? Payroll? Yearly licenses and fees? Include all of these items on your budget.

When you've totaled your expenses, compare that number to your income. If you've overspent, this is your opportunity to look at where you can cut back. Remember, the little things add up. Try to beat your numbers from last year. This year, you'll be tracking, so you should be more conscious of your spending. Sometimes, just seeing the budget in writing will keep you from overdoing it.

Each month, we run a report that shows what our budget planned for versus what we actually spent. This "budget vs. actual" report is incredibly helpful in providing another snapshot of the business's financial health. It also helps me further develop and hone my budget to be more accurate.

Most people feel that if they stray from their budget at all, they've failed. They see budgets as punishment. That's not what I use them for. I use a budget to get a clear view of what I have to spend, and then I remain flexible. If I need to spend more one month on a big-ticket item, then I cut back a little during the following months to cover it. This way, I help myself stay on track with my financial goals, my savings deductions, and any investments I want to make into my business.

The important thing is that you make a start.

I also create different budgets for each area of our school. Marketing, human resources, and overhead all have their own budgets. Each of these is also listed on a master budget, but dividing the master into departments helps us see each one in light of the goals we have for that area.

Tracking Tools

The final, vital aspect of money management for business owners is a good tracking system. I want to emphasize this here: the important thing is that you make a start.

I took baby steps. First, I used my Walgreens spiral notebook. Then I used Microsoft Word, into which I typed up a list of my expenses and a list of income. Then I used an Excel spreadsheet, which frankly confused the heck out of me for a few months. I switched finally to QuickBooks.

There are many options available at all price points and stages of learning. You can set up a spreadsheet or a Google Drive document to track your finances until you can afford a more sophisticated system. Some quality systems are available for free as well.

Keep in mind that the tracking system shouldn't be so complex that you avoid using it. Ask your accounting advisor for input on what essentials you need for your industry, and start with one report at a time. As you build the habit of tracking, you'll find it a reassuring and empowering process.

SET FINANCIAL GOALS

In 2008, the recession was keeping many good businesses down. All over the country, people were struggling, and our community was no different. However, in spite of the general downturn, my dance school continued to grow. We were teaching 300 students and looking to hire more teachers. I was thrilled with the results we were getting and incredibly grateful for the good fortune. In fact, I was ready to buy my own building.

I decided to have a space custom built for the needs of our school. It was an exciting venture. It wasn't easy to convince a bank to loan us the money—not only was the nation in a recession, but I was also a twenty-three-year-old business owner. Fortunately, our clear record of growth over the previous years, our bank records, and our projections of income for the future won their confidence.

My grandparents helped me find land to build on . . . it was in the middle of nowhere. At the time, land was expensive, and my options were limited. My family's excavation company dug our basement. At our grand opening, the mayor and members of the Oak Creek Chamber of Commerce attended. We planned activities for the kids, invited media representatives, and—of course—showcased dancing.

I kept pinching myself. I couldn't believe that what started as a hobby in my parents' backyard had turned into this enormous endeavor.

Once we were in our new 8,700-square-foot building, our clientele continued to expand. We started attracting students from neighboring towns, students who liked our fun, family-oriented approach to dance. Families from nearby Franklin kept asking us when we were going to open a second location.

I loved the idea of a second location, so I looked at the numbers. Sort of.

I considered how well the first location was doing and saw that it could cover the cost of a rented building in Franklin. I made the decision and rented a space in 2012, opening shortly after.

Let me just say this: I was lucky. The second location grew very quickly, turning a profit within two years, but until it covered its own expenses, I was taking money each month from the first location.

My CPA later sat me down and told me that I had been taking a big risk. His advice was to avoid making the first location suffer for the second one. A profit within two years is rare, and the more likely outcome would have been the first location's being pulled under by the decision to open a second prematurely.

Going forward, as I looked at plans to build our own custom second location, my criteria for making a big investment changed. I made sure that the new investment—or perhaps in your case, the new product or service or division—could stand on its own without being a drain on something else. I looked realistically at how long it would take to turn a profit in the new building, and I used a special savings account set aside for its expenses.

For me, the experience with the second custom studio was not only valuable for teaching me money management, but it was also a lesson in goal setting. Rather than making a big decision based on passion alone, I've learned to set goals that I can attain without harming my existing business.

> With more money, you have even more responsibility to spend it wisely on your business's future.

SPEND ON PAPER FIRST

If you haven't taken time to plan for what you're going to do with the money coming in, now is the time. I used to think that the more money we made, the easier financial goal setting would become. We'd have plenty of money to pay bills, upgrade the studio, and even expand. What could be difficult about that?

The reality is that with more money, you have even more responsibility to spend it wisely on your business's future.

I chose to create milestone goals for myself. For example, at the $10,000 mark, I would upgrade one aspect of the studio. At the $15,000 mark, I would hire front desk help.

I also set monthly financial goals to track our marketing output versus what we expected to pull in revenue. Because I track my numbers monthly, I know whether I'm hitting those goals. If we invest heavily in a new marketing effort one month with the goal to increase clients by 10 percent, and we don't show the increased revenue to go along with that, I know something is wrong. I can stop, reevaluate my goals, and start over.

For startups, financial goal setting is critical because many new entrepreneurs are still working "day jobs" to make ends meet while their businesses get off the ground. If you don't know how much you need to cover all of your expenses—both professional and personal—then you won't know how long you'll need to keep moonlighting.

I waited a long time to pay myself a salary. I know it may seem odd that I wasn't pulling anything out for myself, but I told myself I was saving money for my business this way. In fact, I worked at a local bar and grill on weekends for years after starting my business. The problem was that I hadn't set any financial goals for when this arrangement should end, and I didn't have all the information I needed to make that decision month in and month out.

While I told myself I was saving money by not taking a salary, I was actually spending it on things I didn't really need, like accessories for the studio. If I had set my financial goals with a salary in mind, I would have been saving that money and starting some good habits.

Goal setting is about looking at the reality of your situation, determining where you want to end up, and then connecting the dots so you can get there. If you've skipped this process in the past, it may be part of the reason for your current challenges.

As we move forward together and determine how to save your company in the Business Rescue Roadmap, you'll get a realistic picture of what your business is actually worth and what you think it could be worth in the future. That's goal setting.

SIGN POSTS

For your business to survive and thrive, you're going to have to face your money challenges head on. You don't have to solve everything at once. Take baby steps toward money mastery, and give yourself credit for the little victories.

Consult a CPA if you haven't already. If you do have one on board, set an appointment to go over your areas of struggle. Go on. Send an email, or pick up the phone and set an appointment now.

Having knowledge about financial tools and practices doesn't do you any good if you don't use them. A budget that you never consult is worthless. Take a little time each month for a financial update. It's amazing how much difference an hour can make.

The more money you earn, the more challenges you will have. If you're putting off dealing with money habits until you have a surplus, give up that fantasy. Managing the small amount will prepare you for managing the larger one.

CHAPTER FOUR

My first piece of business marketing was a handwritten flyer on an 8½ x 11-inch sheet of paper. The flyer listed my name along with the time, date, and place of my first dance group meeting. I didn't think of my dance team as a business back then, so I wasn't even aware of terms like avatar, graphic design, or tagline.

I was aware, subconsciously, of my target audience, even if I didn't call it that.

I hung the flyers at our local middle school, drawing seventeen students to that first meeting. Today, while I laugh at how naïve I was, I love that messy, amateur flyer more than I can say because it started the business that has grown beyond my dreams and touched the lives of thousands of people.

Now the world sees me in a completely different way. I am not the eighteen-year-old with handwritten flyers. The world sees me as a polished adult with a polished marketing strategy. The problem is that when I talk to people, they get intimidated by the polished adult.

Your brand is your face in the community.

What I want you to hear is that marketing doesn't have to be scary. If you allow yourself to be intimidated by what you perceive as complex, you'll lose valuable opportunities. You'll get stuck, and you'll be left wondering whether your business is worth saving. So let's break this down and make it super simple.

Your brand is your face in the community. Think of it like this:

On a lazy Saturday afternoon, you don't leave your house all day except to check your mail. Now, let's pretend that's the only time your neighbor ever sees you. What does your neighbor think of you? You only own pajamas? You have no friends? Even your cat, who pokes his head out the door with wide eyes, can't wait to escape the lonely, dark cave of a life you lead?

Of course, this isn't accurate. You do yoga every morning in your sunroom. You have a great hobby, like jewelry making or reading biographies. You park your car in the rear of your house and leave five days a week, dressed professionally, with a smile on your face (or at least a cup of coffee in your hand). Your friends meet you for lunch every Wednesday and for happy hour every Friday. You have a great family that lives one town over, and you spend one weekend a month with them. Your life is full and happy.

But all your neighbor sees is a half-dressed, crumpled, solo version of you—because that's all you've ever shown her.

Branding is that trip to the mailbox. It's the only thing that most people will ever see of your business. Let's take some time to evaluate where you can dress up your image.

EVALUATE YOUR BRAND

When people first started talking to me about my brand, my eyes glazed over. I'd heard the word, but I thought of a brand name or logo. I did not think of a list of characteristics.

Your brand is so much more than the name of your company. It's your attitude, your values, and your identity. My mentor always says your brand is everything people can interact with, see, touch, taste, feel, and hear about your business.

A brand evaluation is a process too long to describe in this book, but I can give you some places to start. I'll also give you a step-by-step plan for brand analysis in the marketing section of the Business Rescue Roadmap.

First, step back and take an objective look at the name of your company.

When we outgrew the first rented studio and were moving into a larger custom building, I wanted to change our name. Studio 21 just didn't fit the size of our operation or the goals I had for the business. Eventually, The Academy of Performing Arts became our official name, but I only landed on that after much consideration not only about who we were at that point but also about who we wanted to be.

Does your brand name match the vision you have for your business, or are you stuck on something from your startup days or your first catchy idea?

Next, look at your tagline and other language surrounding your brand name. Perhaps you have a slogan on your packaging or a tagline on your website. Just because this branding worked when you first started the company, that doesn't mean it will still work. Evaluate how effective it is as you consider the vision for your company and the perspectives of new clients.

Finally, make a list of adjectives that describe your business. Are you family friendly and fun? Professional and polished? Do your customers describe you as reliable or prompt or innovative? Think about how you want to be perceived, and be sure your brand reflects that on all levels. Be sure to consider your business's values and mission.

Remember, your brand needs to be consistent, and it should reflect a specific, clear, and realistic view of who you are as a company.

CONSIDER YOUR AUDIENCE

When you make a phone call, do you ever just dial a number but not know who you're going to be talking to? No, because that would be silly. You speak to people knowing who they are. Your brand is no different.

What I've learned about evaluating your brand is that you can't be everything to everyone. The further along I got in my business, the more I realized I was trying to do just that. With only a couple competitors in our area, I was trying to offer clients the same services and experiences as those other studios. I felt like I needed to keep up with them to be competitive and to hang on to clients.

Then I started hearing complaints from our customers. We even lost business. Customers came to me and said, "I thought we would get such and such, and we didn't." Some customers felt I wasn't delivering what they expected—what my marketing materials had promised.

It was about this time that I heard about the concept of a client avatar, and everything clicked. I had never taken the time to consider the people I could serve and how they feel, think, and behave.

CREATE YOUR AVATAR

Who's your ideal customer? Think in terms of specific people. If you've been saying that all of America would like your toothpaste for sensitive, yellowed teeth because all Americans brush their teeth, you're missing the benefit of this exercise. Yes, I'm sure most of America would like resilient, white teeth, but only a fraction of them are actually interested in making a purchase toward that end.

Ask yourself the details of your ideal client's life and identity. Is it a man or a woman? How old? Married, divorced, single? What's her age? Does she have kids, grandkids, a book club? Does she work, and if so, where? What are her fears, her hopes, her dreams for the future?

Be as specific as you can. You can even name your avatar.

Once we had established the avatar of our ideal customer, everything changed. Now, when someone comes in or calls the front desk, we find out what she's looking for. Does she want her child to take dance for several hours a day? Is she envisioning the show *Dance Moms*? If so, we tell her we don't think we're the right studio for her family. We turn her away.

Rather than costing me money, this has helped me retain customers and increase enrollment. I attract the kind of clients who are looking for exactly what we offer.

When coming up with your avatar, it helps to think about what your clients are buying—and then to think *beyond why* they're buying. Our clients are looking for more than just a performance experience for kids. They're looking for care and respect for their children. One of the ways we reinforce that intangible desire is by providing a video that becomes a keepsake.

Ask yourself also what kind of price this person is willing to pay for the experience with you. When looking at pricing structures, most people start out by thinking they want to be on the cheaper end of the spectrum to be competitive within their market. I started out that way.

Then I examined the results I was getting. I offered the lowest prices, but I had constant complaints and difficulties with clients who were there because of that low fee. Instead, as I looked at my client avatar, I realized I wanted to attract someone who was willing to pay a higher price to get a better-quality experience.

Ever since I raised my rates—offering more value and additional items—I've had fewer customer complaints and happier dancers.

By tailoring your offering
to your avatar, you
increase the chances
of creating something
she really wants and
is willing to pay for.

Review your offering through the eyes of your avatar. Now that you have a specific person in mind, ask yourself whether she would be happy with your product or service, its pricing, its benefits, its customer service, and its add-on sales. By tailoring your offering to your avatar, you increase the chances of creating something she really wants and is willing to pay for.

UNDERSTAND MEDIA

Once you know who you're marketing to—your avatar—tailor your messaging to reach her. Start by figuring out where she is. Is she at the coffee shop on her phone all the time? Reading a parenting magazine? Watching the local news each night?

Wherever she is, you need to be there.

If you're on the Internet and can sell your product to anyone, anywhere, you're fortunate. I have a brick and mortar and can't sell my service to anyone farther than about fifteen miles from our locations. My advertising focuses on our regional families, so I do very little online marketing.

I've established advertising relationships with all of the local magazines and newspapers in my area. If you're interested in working with print or online magazines, local television, or other local media, a press release process is a necessity.

Start by building a list of people to whom you want to spread the message about your business. If you're a real estate agent, maybe you want your local newspaper to profile your community efforts or you want a city magazine to write a blurb on your sales award with a national real estate association. Whatever the case, you'll need newsworthy items to share. Just bragging about your service or product doesn't pass muster with editors and producers.

When you've created a list, it's time to get that message in front of the viewer. A great way to do that is with a good, old-fashioned press release, which never dies. Your goal is to put together a story that focuses on the value for the viewer or reader. Remember when you put out your press release that each media outlet also has an ideal audience—again, the client avatar. They are marketing to a specific person, so write your release to interest that person. If you're sending it to a parenting magazine, emphasize the benefits to families and kids. If you're sending a press release to a local fashion website, emphasize the beauty perks that visitors could receive as a result of your story.

Expect rejection. Not every press release you send is going to be picked up as a story by that media outlet. However, by sending it to ten or twenty people on a list, you increase your odds.

When you are writing your press release, look at examples online. Keep

Read a sample press release that got me great exposure at StacyTuschl.com/ Tools.

in mind the number-one rule: it's not all about you. Your press release is about what you're doing and how that's interesting to the media outlet's avatar.

The online world is an extension of old school print and broadcast. It's a faster, more immediate form of communication, but it also has an avatar.

For more online advertising outlets, go to StacyTuschl.com/Tools.

In terms of advertising online, there are many options—from group forums to blogs to industry websites. I'll give you three great places to start.

1. Social media is the biggest opportunity for marketing, in most cases. We have a few social media accounts for our business, and I place periodic ads on these sites. Target the ads to a specific audience and area.

2. Your website is usually the first place people visit—even before your brick-and-mortar location, if you have one. This is a crucial place to invest some money and make the site live and breathe your brand.

3. A blog is another way to reach your client avatar and position yourself as an expert. Provide helpful suggestions and information that your client avatar would be interested in reading.

In general, repeat the same messaging through multiple channels. Let me give you an example.

Say we have an event coming up—maybe a dance event that benefits a local charity—and we want to spread the word. We develop a graphic that advertises the event. Then we use that graphic as an image on our homepage, on our social media pages, and on a postcard direct mailer or flyer at local businesses such as daycares. We could also use it for a social media ad or boosted post to ensure that more people see it. This multichannel approach helps us get the most from our graphic design budget and hit a larger audience than we would by using only one of these channels.

MARKET ON THE CHEAP

"I don't have any money for marketing." I hear this all the time, and my answer is always the same: "You don't need any." Today, start-ups and businesses with low marketing budgets have far more options than businesses starting out ten or fifteen years ago did. When I began my dance business, handwritten flyers were the height of my no-cost marketing.

Today, we can use social media to create a free online presence. Consider which channels work best for your particular company. If you want to show photos of your business or products while you interact with followers, you probably need a page that doesn't limit your word count. If posting how-to pictures is important, look for a site that is geared toward images rather than words. Other sites are aimed at starting conversations with people in your industry. Social media is only effective if you choose the right site for the right content.

You can also use free graphic design tools to create polished marketing material.

If you sell products, look into places where you might build on other people's existing efforts. Farmers' markets, Etsy, and shopping booth malls are all great options for free or low-rent presences.

Before you start spending any significant money on marketing, test out your plan. My first big marketing effort was to purchase 10,000 door hangers for about $100. I designed and hand delivered each one of those door hangers. Let me say that I am not a designer, so these weren't the most attractive door hangers. They got the message across, though, and I attracted new clients thanks to that marketing strategy.

Discover more examples of how to use a multichannel marketing strategy at StacyTuschl.com/ Tools.

As I've said before, it's okay to start small. In fact, in many cases, it's the smart thing to do. Your risk is low, and your return may surprise you. When you complete the Business Rescue Roadmap in chapter 7, I'll help you determine where to start and how to do it in baby steps.

RESEARCH YOUR COMPETITORS

As you begin creating a marketing strategy—whether it's an image for your free Facebook page or a large-scale media campaign—it's important to research your competition first.

Strong competitors are a good thing. They show there is a healthy market for your product or service. Don't be afraid to learn from what they're doing. The idea here isn't to look better than everyone else does, but to look different. You want to show how you stand out from the others.

I now focus on emphasizing the differences in our marketing messaging. Showing how we're different from the other studios doesn't mean we're better. It just means we're better suited to certain students than other studios are.

For my list of free and low-cost business tools, visit StacyTuschl.com/Tools.

A marketing example I love is Drybar. They market to a different audience from standard hair salons because they really do offer a unique experience. Drybar looked at what was being done in the industry, and they put a new twist on it by exclusively offering a blowout. They knew some women didn't need to get a haircut or color, but they did want to get their hair blown out—without paying a crazy amount of money.

If you have the same basic product or service as everyone else does, and you can't figure out what makes you different, then it's time to reevaluate. Think about what you can add or change that will bring some unique aspect to your offering.

Find out where your competitors are placing their marketing efforts. Do they rely heavily on social media? If so, how many followers do they have, and how often do they post? What kinds of posts on their timelines get the most likes, shares, or comments?

If they use direct mail, look at what kinds of deals they're offering. How often do they send out mailers? Do the same research with print or online advertising.

Keep in mind that you don't necessarily have to advertise using the same channels as your competition does. Just because they're using direct mail frequently doesn't mean it's working for them and giving them results that translate into sales. Most of your competition isn't even tracking how people heard about their businesses, so they may not know whether their ad is effective.

Before you commit any large sum of money or huge amount of time to a marketing strategy—even one that your competitors use successfully—test it. Start small. See what percentage of people respond favorably. Then note how many of those responses actually turn into clients. Tweak your messaging if necessary. Add a different coupon or post during different times of the day.

And for heaven's sake, be sure to include a big call to action.

INSPIRE YOUR AUDIENCE TO ACT

The number-one mistake people make in creating marketing messaging is not including a call to action.

This statement tells people what you want them to do next. Of course, to write a good call to action, you need to know what you want people to do in response to your ad.

> The number-one mistake people make in creating marketing messaging is not including a call to action.

Do you want them to visit your website? Call for an appointment? Schedule a free quote? Once you figure this out, write a sentence directing people to do just that.

For example, if we send out a mailer, we include a coupon or a request to bring the mailer in for a reward of some kind. It might say, "Bring this in for 20% off a class package," or, "Mention this ad when you call, and get your first class free."

A call to action is a key element in your ability to track your advertising results. If your prospects aren't inspired to take action after they see your ad, how will you know they saw it? How will you know whether it was effective? For every piece of marketing I put out there, I make sure there is some way to track it.

Train your customer service representatives to ask prospects how they heard about your business—but don't stop there. Most people see an ad multiple times before they take any action. Maybe your new client saw you at a local event, read a news story about you in the local paper, saw an ad in a magazine, and then saw a flyer at the neighborhood coffee shop. Which one triggered her to actually take action and call you?

Ask your prospect what inspired her to come in or call. You want to know specifically what worked and why.

Same thing with social media posts. Which ones are resulting in click-throughs to your website? Which ones are being shared and resulting in more followers? (Don't forget your call to action: "click here" or "share this.")

TRACK OUTCOMES

No amount of marketing will work long term without effective tracking. The event that works one season won't work in another. The ad that helps sell one product won't move a related product at all. The post that people share a hundred times on one social media outlet will fall flat on another.

I've found that to have effective, long-term marketing results, you need effective, long-term tracking systems in place to monitor what's working and what's not.

Your marketing strategies should be measurable. Start with a customer-management system to track leads as well as existing clients. Collect some kind of contact information on every person who reaches out to you, comes across you at an event, or receives one of your marketing pieces.

I'm going to offer you some goals to shoot for in this area, and they don't have to be complicated. In the beginning, I kept tally on sticky notes. From there, I upgraded to a Microsoft Excel spreadsheet. After a few years, I bought a full-blown software tracking system that gave me a million different reports. No matter what state you're in with your tracking system—or lack of it—don't worry; start where you are and know that there's room to grow.

If you're asking how people hear about you and what made them contact you, you're gathering a lot of basic information you'll need for tracking. With this data alone, you can track month to month whether you're getting most of your referrals from flyers, ads, or social media. You'll know whether people are finding you by driving by or through recommendations from existing clients. And you'll be able to see whether your social media or other online advertising dollars are worth the investment.

For social media, most major platforms have analytics so you can see who is following you and what kind of engagement you're getting. It's imperative that you pay attention to this data, especially if you're sched-uling your posts and having someone else respond to any comments.

If your post about a weekly pricing special only got fifty likes but your post about your new puppy got 150 likes, you will want to know whether this is a fluke or a trend. Do your customers prefer it when you post personal pictures and funny comments? Or do they usually click more on coupons? You'll find this information in your analytics.

If you're running social media ads, monitor the results through the social media site. In addition, with ads, you can place a link directly to your own website; your website analytics will show you a lot of good information.

On the back end, be sure you're tracking the sales that resulted from those clicks. If you have a good call to action, then you're sending people from your online ads and social media posts to your website. You can track how many times that happens. Beyond that, record how much your sales rise after a marketing effort begins. Followers, likes, and click-throughs are great, but if they aren't translating into profits, you need to make some changes.

I suggest that you create a marketing strategy. For example, post twice a day on one social media site for a month. Set a start and end date, and then follow the analytics to see how much website traffic comes from that outlet. Track how much your revenue rises during that spe-cific period. These stats help you see how effective your marketing plan is in real dollars.

To get even more specific, track what times of day get the best responses, which types of posts get the most engagement, and who your primary followers—the ones who interact with you the most—are.

MARKET FOR RETENTION

Okay, you got them in the door. You hung the flyers, posted the valuable social media content, and sent out a killer press release. Now what? If you think your marketing ends when clients walk through the door, think again.

When I raised my prices, I didn't just raise them for the sake of having premium prices. I raised them to offer a more valuable service. I'm the highest-priced studio in my area, but we offer one of the best experiences, and a big part of that is our strategy to market for client retention.

Clients are loyal for many reasons, but the primary one is how you make them feel. Your products and services need to be good quality, of course, and you need to offer good customer service when someone has a problem. You probably need to be convenient, set your prices correctly, and share similar values with your clientele. But the way you make your clients feel is an intangible ingredient in customer retention that many entrepreneurs miss.

If you put your focus on making your clients feel the love and appreciation that you have for them, you'll be amazed how far these efforts go. People like getting bonuses and receiving extras throughout the year—things your cheaper competitors can't offer.

Let me take you through some examples of these little bonuses and extras.

When you're shopping around for a new daycare for your child, let's say you call three different places. Now imagine that one daycare calls back and offers you a tour. Another one doesn't return your call—ever. The third sends your child a little sticker book and coloring page with a note that was addressed to just to him—and they send along a brochure for you. Which one are you more likely to go with?

Another idea is to offer a money-back guarantee, free trial, or sample.

I used to hesitate to do this. Then one day I was at a conference, and someone said to me, "If you sold a product, and, after trying it, the client just hated it and thought it was the worst product ever, would you refund her money?" Of course, my answer was yes. "Well then," the person said, "why aren't you advertising that? Why don't you have a money-back guarantee? Why aren't you reassuring people that you'll do whatever you can to make it right if something goes wrong?"

In a sense, a free trial is the same thing. If a new client were to dislike our classes, I would give her money back anyway. But if she does like her experience with us, then she's likely to become a loyal customer.

Welcome gifts are a great bonus people don't expect. Don't just wine and dine them before they become customers. Continue to surprise them. For example, let's say you own a fitness center. Once your customer signs up, give her a welcome gift that includes a cute bag for carrying her gym shoes or workout clothes. This little gift doesn't have to cost much, but it immediately shows that you intend to make the new client feel special.

Make your clients feel special.

After a few weeks of classes, reach out to each client by phone and ask about her experience. So often, people are wooed into doing business with a company . . . and then they never hear from that business again. You want your clients to know you value them even after you have their business—in fact, you should value them even more. So show it. This little phone call can also save a few clients from leaving because it gives them the opportunity to talk about issues they probably wouldn't have brought to you otherwise. Most people are generally shy about complaining. Instead of complaining, they just leave. But if you open the conversation, you may discover challenges that can be overcome before they turn into failed relationships.

This works for any industry. Think about the dentist who has headphones so you can listen to your favorite radio station, the flower shop that also delivers a personalized teddy bear to a new mother, or the bakery that creates a special family seating area with kid-sized tables and chairs. What can you do in your industry that will set you apart?

You can afford to do all of these things for your clients because you are charging a quality fee for a quality experience. I realize not every business can put on these kinds of events or directly give something to every customer, but the key is to think about how you can make your clients feel special—how you can give them something tangible to express your intangible gratitude for their loyalty.

EXERCISE CAUTION

I mentioned earlier that many entrepreneurs get grand ideas for how to market their businesses, and then they sit paralyzed because they can't afford that dream strategy. The other side of this picture is a business owner who throws too much money at an unproven or extravagant marketing plan, only to harm the business by stretching the finances too thin to make ends meet.

I caution you to be realistic. Build up slowly. If money is tight, cut back on your marketing budget, and use the free tools I talked about earlier. Don't feel like you have to bite this entire apple at once. Yes, it's shiny and exciting to think about all the ways you can spread the word about your business, but marketing is an ongoing process.

You'll have plenty of time to experiment with other strategies, but not if you spend all your money on a failing marketing plan and drive your company out of business.

If you feel over your head in this area, or if you have your sights set on something bigger than what you are qualified to oversee, outsource.

We've outsourced to a graphic designer for a few years now. Recently, we hired an in-house marketing person, but before that, we frequently used freelance help. You can hire an agency, but in my opinion, the days of large marketing agencies for small businesses are nearly over. With all of the freelancing sites and outsourcing organizations available, there's no need to pay top dollar to a large agency when you can get great work for a more reasonable fee paid to one person.

However, keep in mind that just because your materials are professionally designed, it doesn't mean they will get results. You must track all materials, regardless of who created them.

Marketing needs will change; be ready to change with them. If you've been in business for a while, don't feel discouraged if you don't have this area down pat yet. It took me five years before I really looked at our marketing and the concept of an avatar. The point is this: start small, but start now.

SIGN POSTS

Remember that marketing is the only aspect of your business that some people will ever see. This vital area is often left out of early budgets or put to the side when things get busy. Make marketing a priority, and you'll discover the enormous impact it has on your business's well-being.

1. Now that you've thought about your brand, ask for others' opinions. Bring in key players or ask trusted advisors for their opinion of how your business name, logo, and other marketing efforts reflect your values and brand as a whole.

2. Be sure you're focusing your marketing efforts where they work. The first place you should aim is your pool of existing clients. Then seek out prospects where they are, and save your marketing for those targeted areas or media outlets.

3. Even if you've never written a description of your customer avatar before, take time now to write some ideas in your journal. Who is she? Is she married, a mother, a business owner? Does she worry about saving money, looking professional, or staying fit? What is it she hopes to get from buying your service or product? Sketch her out, and then add more to this list when you get to the Business Rescue Roadmap in chapter 7.

CHAPTER FIVE

I love teaching dance, but teaching was going to kill my business. I started the dance school as a volunteer because I enjoyed teaching and sharing my passion for dance with others. I wasn't in it for the money, but after incorporating my little hobby, moving into a rented studio space, and attracting more than one hundred dancers, I realized I was officially running a business.

Actually, my business was running me.

I was the front desk person, operations manager, teacher, bookkeeper, janitorial service, marketing department, and sales force.

Yes, I had gotten advice from my family members who were experienced at running a company of their own. Yes, I had a professional accountant on board to help me with some financial requirements. But really, I was doing just about everything else myself.

While I was doing it all at work, I wasn't seeing my family and friends. I couldn't enjoy other hobbies, learn new skills, or travel. I didn't get enough rest, eat healthy foods, or take care of my mental health by having regular down time. My entire life suffered because my business was driving me instead of the other way around.

There was no way I could sustain that kind of lifestyle for long. Ultimately, it would have led me to exhaustion and the inevitable question: "Is this business even worth saving?"

So I hired two teachers. Then I hired a front desk person to help with managing the day-to-day operations—in fact, I hired my sister. These additional staff members alleviated some of the stress I was under, but not all of it.

Having more teachers and a front desk person meant that I could offer more classes. Which meant that we attracted more students. Which meant there was even *more* work to do behind the scenes.

People often think that the bigger your business gets, the easier it becomes to run. You might think, "If I only had 50 more customers . . . if I only had $10K more in revenue . . . things would be so much easier." What you don't realize is that your challenges don't disappear as your business grows. In fact, they grow with your business. If you keep doing what you're doing—but doing more of it—you'll get the same results on a bigger scale.

If you keep doing what you're doing—but doing more of it—you'll get the same results on a bigger scale.

On top of all of the demands of a growing business, I was still teaching dance classes. The finances, vendor relationships, marketing, human resources, and vision and planning involved in growing a business—all of these areas were suffering because I spent multiple hours each week either teaching dance or preparing to teach dance. These were hours that the business needed my attention to be healthy and thriving.

I realized, finally, that if I spent my time teaching, I was going to kill the business.

Once again, I found myself in the position of being run by my business. The task list far outweighed my strength in terms of time and personal resources. Teaching was eating up my ability to be an entrepreneur.

MAKE THE TOUGH DECISIONS

I had to make a choice: continue doing what I loved and downsize the business to something more manageable, or stop teaching and become a full-time entrepreneur.

Fortunately, for me, I didn't just love teaching—I loved entrepreneurship, too. Starting that company ignited a flame inside me I hadn't known existed before. I loved the visionary aspect of growing a company, the ownership and sense of accomplishment that comes with each new milestone, and the joy that my business was bringing to the people involved.

So I stopped teaching.

It wasn't easy at first. And yes, I missed it. But because my passion lay with the business as a whole, I felt confident in my choice.

I wish I could say this was the last time I struggled with letting the business run me, but I think we all encounter this experience each time our business grows to a new level. We get too many clients to handle all the orders, we have too many prospects to make all the sales calls, our marketing needs outgrow our skill sets, or we start earning so much money that we no longer understand what to do with it.

The end goal should be that your business runs itself.

Whatever the cause of your business growth, the stress and responsibilities that come with it can run you down if you don't take a step back and grab the wheel again.

If I had kept teaching rather than stepping back to run the business, I would not have the number of students I do today, nor would I have the beautiful facilities we're in now, because I wouldn't have generated the revenue to support something this big. By doing everything on my own, I would have made my dream a lot smaller—and gotten burned out a lot faster in the process.

I don't know about you, but when I'm burned out, I don't have time or mental energy to come up with new ideas, much less implement them. My relationships suffer, my health declines, and I lose my passion—the very thing that made me want to be in the business in the first place.

The goal should be that your business runs itself. You should be able to take a vacation, take maternity leave, start a new venture, or spend time doing whatever else you please because your business is self-sufficient, even when you're not in the immediate picture.

I'm not saying you have to build a business that can run without you permanently. Many people love being involved in the daily operations of their companies and have no desire to step away. But even those people need to think about what would happen to their businesses if something happened to prevent them from showing up every day.

If you feel understaffed, worried about clients who don't have anyone else to turn to except you, or incapable of taking a week off without checking messages, then I'm sorry to tell you that your business is running you. And it's time to make a change.

DELEGATE OR ELSE

I call running a business "controlled chaos." Whether it's the building alarm going off in the middle of the night or an employee calling in sick, there are always unexpected demands on my time. If I want to enjoy my life, spend uninterrupted time with my family, and do the other things I love, I have to be in charge of when I work.

This means I have to delegate. I can't be the only one who is available to fill in for another teacher—and today, I'm not. I haven't taught a class in years, but that transition took a long time to complete.

Like most people, I thought no one could do the job as well as I could. I'm not saying I was the best dance teacher in the state of Wisconsin, but between the cost of another employee and the time I'd have to invest in training her, it seemed simpler and more economical to do all of the teaching myself.

The problem is that I was also doing a million other things. I wasn't giving teaching my all anymore. My focus was constantly split.

By hiring someone else to teach and fully relinquishing that responsibility, I gave our students a teacher who was 100 percent focused on teaching. My clients are happy, and my stress is lower.

Sure, there are things you can actually do better than other people can. But ask yourself, "Am I doing them better than someone else, or am I multitasking myself into mediocrity?" If you're only giving half of yourself to some of your tasks that could be delegated, then why not delegate them?

Every entrepreneur has those $10-an-hour tasks. Whether it's handing out fliers, making calls, or doing online research, if you haven't delegated these tasks to an assistant, then *you* are the assistant doing the $10-an-hour work. If I have a marketing piece I need to mail out, and I find myself placing stamps and licking envelopes on past-due invoices instead of focusing on marketing, I'm not delegating properly.

I suggest that you make a list of those $10-an-hour tasks. Write down everything you can think of that could be delegated to someone else.

Make this list with the idea that someone else in your organization could do it better than you, if for no other reason than she will be focused only on that one task. We'll work more on this list in the Business Rescue Roadmap to help pinpoint how you can create new positions and delegate.

If you don't already have someone on staff who can do these things, then review your budget. Where could you cut $300 or $500 from your monthly expenditures and move it to a new team member? Hiring someone part-time or virtually is a great way to start this delegation habit.

As your business grows, you'll delegate more and more. I highly recommend that you keep control over marketing and your checkbook. I hire someone to contribute ideas and execute on marketing, but I offer the guiding vision and the final say. I regularly review my financials, regardless of who is helping me organize them.

OUTSOURCE AS NEEDED

A decade ago, entrepreneurs were forced to struggle to find local help. Today, websites offer professional helpers with varying degrees of experience. Outsourcing is so easy and—in many cases—so reasonably priced that I don't think anyone should make the excuse that she can't afford to get help. I've gone online and hired someone for $15 to do something small, and it was completed in an hour.

Find my list of outsourcing websites at StacyTuschl.com/Tools.

One area in which many entrepreneurs need help early on is customer service. When clients have questions or challenges, they need on-demand help to assist them. Answering endless emails and phone calls doesn't allow you to focus on growing the business, which is your number-one task.

In the beginning, I outsourced customer service to an agency that answered the phone for me using my company's greeting. Then they told the caller that the person who could best address their question was out of the office, would be back at such-and-such a time, and would be happy to return the call then. This simple service was so much better than allowing a client to call in only to hear a voice mail message. If the caller was a prospective client, I had instructed the service to call me right away so I could immediately jump on that sales call. The entire service only cost about $30 a month. It worked great for me because I could provide myself with some much-needed time away from the phone in the mornings, and my prospects and clients were still getting personal attention.

In addition to adding skill sets and time into your company mix, one of the biggest benefits to delegation and outsourcing is the ability it gives you to be present for your life. What if you have a funeral to attend? A birthday to plan? A romantic date night? Do you step out to take a phone call? It's time to truly unplug and be present for those you love.

There have been times in my career when I have had to take time off—sometimes for a few months at a time. Thankfully, I had already implemented a system of delegation and outsourcing so this was possible without harming the business. Give yourself permission to be human and have a life.

MANAGE YOUR CRAZY SCHEDULE

As entrepreneurs, we constantly have appointments, challenges, questions, and demands coming at us. Fortunately, we have phones today that allow us to manage most of our business needs on the go.

Sometimes, though, this little gadget attached to your hand at all times doesn't make you feel very fortunate. It can make you feel like a slave to your schedule. Running from one appointment to the next, returning calls during your commute, trying to squeeze in every last meeting that anyone requests—not to mention all the personal errands and appointments you've got to keep up with—is enough to make you want to chuck it all some days.

Let me tell you what I've learned. The people who are truly thriving in their businesses are the ones who have learned to tame those demands. And by "tame," I mean that these people have learned to reduce the demands on their time by managing well.

It took me a long time to learn this lesson. In the beginning, my insane schedule didn't even leave me time for the basics.

One fall, I was so busy that I didn't have time for a hair appointment—I didn't have the money either, honestly—so I bought a box of hair color from the drugstore and did it myself. Unfortunately, I didn't test it first, and I had a bad reaction. Bad as in silver-and-purple hair. This was before colored streaks were cool, let me tell you. The worst part is that I was so insanely busy, and my schedule was so out of my control, that it took me three days to stop working and see my hairdresser to have this fixed. I had zero time for myself. Instead, I wore a hat. I know my team thought I had gone a little loopy.

Since then, I've done what I have seen other successful entrepreneurs doing.

First, they have a good calendar. I'm amazed at the number of business owners or consultants who don't use a good calendar system. They run late all the time and forget appointments! They're only human. Anyone would forget a few details here and there, and that's why a scheduling system is critical.

I use Google calendar, but there are plenty of options available. The best calendars will sync your laptop, desktop, phone, and tablet so when you make changes to your calendar on one device, the change shows on all the other ones as well.

I like Google calendar because it's free (a perk!) and it connects to my Gmail account. Let me give you a quick rundown of some ways I use my calendar that may be a little different from how other people use theirs.

First, everything in my calendar is blocked out. I use it to schedule both my professional and my personal time. Every waking hour is filled with something, even if it's "downtime with husband."

I do this because, as I said before, there was a stage of my business life when my time with friends and family was sacrificed to make more room for business. I don't want to let this happen again. I make an intentional effort to protect that personal time. If I were to leave these spaces blank, I would glance at the calendar, think, "Oh, I have this whole evening free," and book a meeting during that time. Instead, I block it out for my personal needs. It helps me emotionally, physically, and spiritually. And in the end, that helps my business, too.

Check out my list of vetted calendar systems at StacyTuschl.com/Tools.

This means I don't have a separate calendar for my child's playdate schedule or my dentist appointments. My workout, lunch hour, trip to daycare to pick up my child—all of it is in my calendar right alongside my business obligations.

Next, I use my calendar to manage my social media posts. I don't use social media for my personal life much, but I know people who do. Some business owners are active on social media sites daily, and that's fine if it works for you and your business. But be sure you use your calendar to schedule that time posting.

The trap people fall into is thinking they will hop onto a social media site for a few minutes to post something or check their newsfeed. You know what happens, right? They look up and an hour has gone by while they liked, shared, and commented on a bunch of entertaining but irrelevant content. Meanwhile, their books aren't balanced, their calls aren't returned, and their team is waiting for the plan.

So visit social media if you like, but schedule a fifteen-minute block of time to do it, and then close it up.

The next item vital to my business focus and success is a block of time scheduled into my calendar for email. There was a time in my early business when I felt like I was becoming addicted to my emails. Seriously, I was checking my phone countless times during the day to see what the latest message said. I couldn't look at that little message number and not check it.

To remove the temptation, I don't have social media or email access on my phone. Instead, I schedule time each day to sit down at my desk, read emails, and respond to them. Today, I feel confident in the responses I send. I'm not a slave to my phone in public or during meals. As a bonus, I've trained people to wait for me.

Let me explain: When I was picking up my phone at all hours of the day, I was often dashing off a response to emails as they arrived. I thought I was being productive and people would appreciate my responsiveness. Instead, what started to happen was that everyone expected me to respond immediately. If they didn't hear back from me right away, they got annoyed. I had trained them to expect that.

If you're getting 200 emails a day, you're not delegating.

Now people know that I will respond within a reasonable twenty-four-hour time period. Of course, if it's urgent, they know to call me instead of sending email. When I started this new procedure, I put a note in my email signature that let people know the specific hours I check email so they could gauge whether they needed to contact me in another way.

My preference is to check email once a day—twice is the maximum. If this sounds too scary for you, do what I did. I started by checking it three times a day: once in the morning, once in the afternoon, and once in the evening. It was hard to let go of the habit and only check email those three times, but after a while, I enjoyed the freedom I felt being away from it. I could be fully present in between my scheduled email times. Next, I cut out the morning session. Turns out that if you check your email in the morning, people expect you to act on that email the same day, and they respond multiple times, creating those never-ending email threads. By stopping email responses in the morning, I took control of my to-do list for that day.

Now I spend much less time on email and get that in-box down to zero every day—it's crazy how fast you can crank them out when you're on the computer to do one specific thing—and I've never felt more productive.

One final note on email: If you're getting 200 emails a day, you're not delegating. Create an organizational structure so everyone on staff knows who to go to for questions and problems. It can't always be you.

A third way I use my calendar is to schedule recurring meetings with all of my staff members who work directly under me. I started this process because I had an employee who would email every time she thought of something. A new idea, a question, whatever, and I'd get another email from this person. Then I scheduled a weekly meeting with her on Mondays.

On Google calendar, there is a task list feature. I asked this employee to start using that task list to create an agenda for her to use at our Monday meetings. I told her that unless it was urgent, she shouldn't email me. She should just add her thought or question to the task list on our calendar appointment.

The next time I received an email from her, I told her I knew the matter she emailed about was important, but it wasn't urgent, so I would talk with her about it on Monday.

I trained her to prioritize, and I reduced my email in-box at the same time. After a few weeks, her emails to me stopped altogether, and our Monday meetings were incredibly productive for us both.

In the Business Rescue Roadmap, I have created a worksheet for you to complete this calendar system upgrade in one day—or one afternoon, depending on how quickly you work. Trust me when I say that taking the time to do this essential step will transform the face of your workday. When you create a calendar system, you will find yourself freed up from the worry and stress that often steal your focus and your passion.

ACT ON YOUR PRIORITIES

When I was writing this book, I almost called this section "Setting Boundaries." For me, setting boundaries means acting on priorities.

This wasn't always the case.

Three years into my business, I had my studio phone line forwarded to my cell phone because I knew I was going to be away from the office, and I didn't want to miss a single prospective client call.

Why was I going to be away from the studio? I was getting married.

Yep, I answered client calls on my wedding day. One hour before I was about to walk down the aisle, I was taking calls, agreeing to mail out information packets, and recording credit card numbers for enrollment. The people on the phone had no idea that the crazy woman on the other end was standing there in a wedding dress.

I did not have good boundaries in the beginning. Most of us don't. It's a learning process. But once you start to hit a wall with all of that running around and crossover, you begin to see the benefit of prioritizing and then acting on those priorities.

If I suggest to an entrepreneur that she set solid boundaries around her time in the morning when she works on marketing ideas, she might give me a million reasons why she can't step away from her email, phone, or team. To all of these, I would ask her, "What are your priorities?"

Setting boundaries means acting on priorities.

This can be a confusing question for some people. In the case of the entrepreneur above, she might answer that she's not sure. Monitoring her team's performance is important to her. So is answering her emails in a timely manner. So also are all of the sales calls she needs to return. She also wants to devote some serious time to revamping her marketing campaign, but how does she set boundaries to get that done when she can't choose a priority?

I've told my team that if someone shows up late to a meeting, we still end on time. I don't do this because I'm trying to cut people short or leave unfinished business. I do this because I respect other people's time as much as I respect my own. I know what my priorities are for that day. I can set a boundary because I know I have a vital task I need to complete or an important appointment that must be kept later that day. My boundaries are inspired by my priorities.

I'm going to talk more about goal setting in chapter 7, but I want to address briefly how this activity applies to your daily schedule and helps you set boundaries—and about the benefits of a good journal.

I always keep my top three yearly goals written in my journal. Because these are big goals, I work backward into action steps that turn into my daily priorities. Every night before I go to bed, I use a journal to write down my top three priorities for the next day. It takes me three minutes. Some of these priorities are time sensitive. Maybe one has to be done tomorrow because an event vendor has given me a due date. Other tasks are related to my big goals, things like a marketing campaign or expansion plan, or other big-picture activities like writing a book. I like to make daily progress toward those goals as much as possible.

Productivity is about quality and not quantity.

I've found that a huge, never-ending to-do list makes people feel defeated and confused. We forget what our priorities truly are, and we get distracted by the effort of checking things off the list. Or, we become so overwhelmed that we quit.

So, every night before you go to sleep, get out your journal and write down three things that you need to get done the next day. Just three. Try it . . . you are worth the three minutes this takes.

Keep in mind that you have to break down big goals into action steps. For example, at one point, my top priorities were to work on this book and create a new website. Obviously, I couldn't achieve either one of these in just one day, so I worked backward from the main objective to discover the smaller goals underneath it. Then I chunked those smaller goals down into actions.

From these actions, I selected the ones that would have the biggest impact. Remember that productivity is about quality and not quantity. I don't want to spend my day taking quick little jabs at a goal. I want to choose something that's really going to help me move forward. I would rather check off one big thing than ten little things.

Once I have my list, I rest easy knowing that when I wake up the next day, I can hit the ground running. Before anything interrupts, before I check email, before I glance at my phone messages, I have my own priorities, and I have set boundaries accordingly.

Once I've completed those three tasks, I create a new top three list to match the time I have available. A three-hour block might be filled with three different actions, but it might also be filled completely by one larger project. For example, maybe I spent three hours brainstorming website taglines, taking a call with my web designer, and browsing the sites of my competitors. Or maybe I spent the entire three hours writing ten pages for my new book.

Things will come up that distract you from your top three to-do items, but that's when your delegation skills come into play. If it doesn't have to do with your main priorities and it can wait, then hand it off or make a note to come back to it. Stay focused on your top three. You'll be amazed at how quickly you move through your list and reach your goals. And you'll be surprised at how easily distracted you were by things that don't really matter.

I also use my journal to time track. How long did I spend on email responses? Do I need to tweak my calendar for that? How many times did I stop for breaks? Did I allow enough time for my commute? All of this information helps me create a calendar that's accurate and in line with my priorities.

And, of course, my journal becomes a great place to jot down notes—
from book suggestions to business ideas.

The fact is that your business is running you because you're letting
it. You are the one in control. It's just a matter of learning how to
take back control and then taking the simple actions to maintain the
control when things threaten to veer off course. Life happens. Problems arise. Staff members leave. You will always have that controlled
chaos when running a business. But your personal relationships, professional reputation, and well-being don't have to suffer along the way.

SIGN POSTS

Are you running your business, or is your business running you? Most women are multitasking masters, but if you're practicing this habit in your business, you're likely drowning in a sea of to-do lists. It's time to take back control by letting go.

1. Delegation and outsourcing are your best bets for reducing the task clutter in your day. Ask yourself why you've put this off in the past. Most people feel they can do tasks better than others can, or they are afraid they can't afford help. Both of these are inadequate excuses when your life is being overrun by your business.

2. Keep a daily journal. This habit has saved my sanity. Write your three daily goals. Write your ideas for new marketing strategies. Write your priorities. Whatever you want to hold dear, remember, or act on goes in your journal.

3. What would you do if your business were self-sufficient, if you could come and go as you pleased, and if you could work only on the projects that interested you? Make a list right now in your journal of the ways in which your life would change.

CHAPTER SIX

At the end of my first year in business, I signed up for a business seminar. I was doing most of the administrative work at my dance school, and I was wearing multiple hats as a business owner. I had hired two teachers, but I was still overwhelmed.

That summer, I sat in a conference room in Brooklyn, New York, with about 250 other business owners. It was the first time I had been with other entrepreneurs, and I was both excited and intimidated by the level of the players in that room.

For me, the wide gap I saw between me and some of those other entrepreneurs made me wonder again, "Is my business was worth saving?

Am I really going to pursue my dance school and raise it to the level I have dreamt it can reach? Am I ever going to be one of the people in this room worth looking up to? Am I willing to do what it will take? Or will I leave this seminar, go home, settle into mediocrity, and eventually—when I am unable to build my business beyond its current limitations—face the failure of my dream?"

Regardless of your product or service, you're in the business of building relationships.

Fortunately, I chose to do what it takes. The first step was trusting someone else to advise me. I had to trust my peers in the industry to share their experiences and opinions. I had to trust strangers I had yet to meet to help me build a team that could realize my goals.

I'm in the people business. So are you. Regardless of your product or service, you're in the business of building relationships. To succeed, you have to surround yourself with the right people. There are businesses that see their customers for one purchase and never see them again, but every business model has the potential to create meaningful relationships in some way.

Most entrepreneurs immediately think of their team when they hear me say this, but I want you to think bigger. We'll talk a lot about how to create a strong team in this chapter, but I'm going to start by calling your attention to relationships that have huge impacts on your success, but that are neglected or overlooked altogether.

FIND A MENTOR

I meet people who balk at this word: mentor. They feel like it implies they are novices. If a grown woman has a mentor, what does that say about her?

In my opinion, it says she's smart. A mentor isn't someone who makes you feel small, stupid, or inexperienced. A mentor is simply someone who has done what you want to do and is willing to talk with you about how she did it. Seeking the help of a mentor sets you above those who are blindly pushing through the unknown by themselves.

Think about this: Would you rather walk through a jungle with a map, a flashlight, and a machete? Or with all of these items *and* a native guide? To me, it's a no-brainer.

Mentorship can be as formal or informal as you like. Some people set up mentorships that meet regularly and follow agendas. Others are more casual and meet as situations arise.

The most important thing is to find someone willing to give you a little of her time. Start in your industry or local business community. Is there someone you admire? A restaurant or retail space you've visited that you liked and respected? Think about what you would like to learn from what that business owner is doing.

You can find mentors at conferences as well. I found my first mentor at a dance industry seminar. Often, there's a sense of legacy at industry conferences. People feel that they were helped by others, and they want to pass that help on to someone else. In general, conference attendees are still learning and growing. This mindset makes them ideal mentors because they can they model lifelong learning, and they will be interested to see what they can learn from you as well.

When you find someone you'd like to talk with about mentorship, think about your approach. I've been asked, "Hey, can we go to lunch so I can pick your brain?" This is essentially like asking, "Hey, can I buy you lunch in exchange for thousands of dollars' worth of free advice and instruction?"

Instead of this one-sided approach, genuinely compliment someone on what you admire about her business. Maybe it's the way she handles customer service or marketing innovations; maybe it's the way she is so honest about her difficult journey to success. Then offer to buy her lunch sometime to talk more. Acknowledge that she is busy, and volunteer to meet her scheduling needs. If she doesn't have time for lunch, ask her a question that will only take five minutes of her time. The clearer you are about what you have in mind, the easier it is for her to say yes if she has some time to offer.

If you click with this person, you can ask her to mentor you on an ongoing basis. This is when you establish how often you'll meet, what you'll discuss, and what you both will glean from the relationship. Keep in mind that you may have something to offer your mentor—maybe technological know-how, consumer feedback, or some other valuable input.

Another option is to hire a professional business coach. If you reach a point in your business life at which you need some objective input over an intense period of time, you'll need a dedicated individual who can guide you through stages of transition or growth. A quali-fied business coach with both education and entrepreneurial experi-ence can make all the difference.

Of course, having a mentor or a coach doesn't mean you can never switch. As you change, your teacher may need to change as well. This can be awkward, but it's doable. If you need help in an area that your mentor can't address, or if you've outgrown your mentor, it's time to switch. Even a business coach can stop learning and growing, leaving you with outdated advice and incomplete information.

Start by thanking your mentor for her time, and then be honest about where you're headed. You don't have to criticize her performance; just tell her you are moving in another direction and have found someone else who can help you with specific areas. A good mentor or coach will be happy that you're growing and will only want the best for you.

Eventually, you can be a mentor yourself. There's no better way to give back to the industry that has helped you succeed.

A mentor isn't the only resource for great advice. Sometimes, the people who are in business alongside you can teach you as well.

CREATE A PEER GROUP

Nobody else is like an entrepreneur. We have very, very different mind-sets from people who aren't compelled to start and run businesses. If you're surrounded by folks who work good (or bad) jobs, report to great (or horrible) bosses, and take home decent (or mediocre) pay-checks, you are denying yourself the benefit of empathetic and experi-enced support.

Someone with a day job is going to have a hard time understanding why you're sacrificing what you are for your business, especially if it's not paying you well yet. You'll face negativity, and you'll probably hear some devil's advocate arguments.

Find entrepreneurs you can talk with regularly. You might find them through industry organizations, social networking, local chamber of commerce events, charitable activities, or seminars. Reach out and shake hands, exchange contact info, and follow up. You'd be surprised at how often the person you think has it all together is also looking for some peer support.

I encourage all entrepreneurs to join a mastermind group. Napoleon Hill introduced the concept of the mastermind group in his book *Think and Grow Rich*, originally published in 1937. Hill defined the peer group as a "coordination of knowledge and effort of two or more people, who work toward a definite purpose, in the spirit of harmony."[1]

Today, there are both free and paid mastermind groups. The paid groups are usually led by experienced business coaches or leaders. Find existing groups online, or form one yourself with a group of like-minded entrepreneurs. When I say like-minded, I don't mean that you should all necessarily be from the same industry or have the same approaches to business. Variety can help you with out-of-the-box thinking. Be sure, though, that all members have the same level of commitment and consistency with their businesses as you do.

I was first introduced to a mastermind group when a fellow entrepreneur contacted me. He had been given my info from our mutual mentor, who thought we would be a good fit. From there, I invited

1 Hill, Napoleon. 1937. *Think and Grow Rich*. Napoleon Hill.

another dynamic entrepreneur I knew would be a great asset to the group. And just like that, we had a mastermind.

In this particular group, we are all in the same industry. This means we can compare P&Ls and balance sheets confidentially, analyze how one school is performing better or worse than the others are, and suggest ways for improvement. Remember to meet with those outside your industry as well, to benefit from their unique view of your processes.

Keep in mind that just because someone owns a business, it doesn't mean she's automatically going to give you great support, feedback, and advice. If you're already successful, someone who hears that you work minimal hours and take vacations all the time may become jealous. Or you may find that while a peer has big goals, she doesn't have the positive attitude and sense of personal responsibility necessary to achieve them. Don't let the negativity of others affect your forward momentum. You may need to weed these people out of your group, but finding the right members can lead to more great referrals, so don't give up.

A good member of a mastermind group is someone who inspires you, gives you honest and respectful feedback, and listens to the same from you. These people are invaluable to both your morale and your success as a business owner. In the Business Rescue Roadmap, I'll help you sort through who belongs in the good influence column and who doesn't.

ATTRACT THE RIGHT CLIENTS

When I started my dance school, I worked with some incredible people. The parents of my first students were encouraging, supportive, and enthusiastic. For the most part, my business has attracted this type of client. They want what we have to offer, and they're happy with our services.

But this isn't always the case. Because of my learning curve as an entrepreneur, or maybe because a client was simply a bad fit, I've had my fair share of difficult customer relationships. As with any analysis of your business, when looking at the quality or quantity of your clients, it's important to start by looking at your own behavior.

Remember that if you're walking out of your house every day in your pajamas and that's all your neighbors ever see, that's all they have to go on in terms of making a judgment about who you are. You'll begin to attract friendships with neighbors who spend most of their time at home in their sweatpants, rather than attracting like-minded business people. You attract what you put out, and you'll turn off people who are looking for something different. Be sure you're sending the right message to the world.

Clients and Your Mission

Do your clients know your company's mission? Most of us learn early to share our mission statement with our team members. We use it as motivation and as a group goal-setting exercise. Do your clients play their own role in that mission?

As a company, we have shared our values and mission with our clients, and we ask them to be responsible for upholding these ideals alongside us. We want them to know what we value and what we expect from ourselves—and from them.

At the beginning of each new relationship, we give the client a copy of our company values and mission statement, and we ask her to agree to uphold these goals with us.

I've found that this creates a great sense of camaraderie among our clients, and it protects the safe, supportive atmosphere at the school. Think of your clients as members of your team. After all, without them, your business can't succeed.

> # Think of your clients as members of your team.

Clients and Your Staff

I tell my staff that their goal is to help our clients. That's our first priority. I also teach my staff to help in the most convenient way for the client.

Make sure that your team knows what's expected of them when interacting with customers. It much easier to keep a client than it is to find a new one. Set your team on the right track by helping them learn great customer service.

When I say that I want to help a client in the most convenient way for her, it means we may ignore a procedure on our end if it helps the client. For example, maybe the policy when someone has a question about billing is for her to contact a certain person during certain hours or to submit her question to a certain email address. But what if the client works during those hours or uses the wrong email address? Rather than make someone who is already at the studio or on the phone with us jump through our policy hoops, we offer to take down the information and get it to the right person.

People want help immediately—always—so another expectation I set with my staff is that we help as fast as we can.

Train your staff to make your clients feel heard, valued, and appreciated—right now.

The last time I tried to cancel a subscription to a magazine, I called the customer service line. I was put on hold for a while. When I talked with an operator, he told me to email the cancellation in-box, so I hung up, wrote an email, and hit send. No response. The next month, my credit card was charged again. When I called back, the operator told me, "I'm sorry, this isn't my department." I just wanted someone to help me get results immediately.

It never seems unreasonable when *you* want it, so be sure not to get resentful when your clients want the same service. Train your staff to make your clients feel heard, valued, and appreciated—right now.

Your Clients and Gifts

Client gifts are one of my favorite things to add into my budget. Whether you're setting aside time or money to show your appreciation for clients, it's a vital step in maintaining your relationships and growing your business.

Start by sending handwritten thank-you notes, making follow-up calls, or offering a loyalty discount. These forms of appreciation go a long way but don't stretch your financial resources much if you're still tight on cash.

As you grow, budget for regular **gifts** throughout the year. At the school, I buy a lot of little thank-you gifts from an online store carrying chocolate-covered berries. Now what if this website sent me one of the packages that I send to my clients with a note that read, "Thanks for being such a loyal customer! Here is a sweet treat to say thank you." Would I be blown away? Would I remain loyal? Absolutely.

Need gift ideas? Read my list of go-to shopping sites at StacyTuschl.com/ Tools.

Remember that most businesses go out of their way to impress prospects and earn clients. But once they've clenched the deal, they may neglect those same people. We all want to feel appreciated, so continue to wow your clients even after you've won them.

Firing Your Clients

You'll usually find the right clients by being clear about who you are as a business and by communicating your services, culture, and mission accurately through your marketing. Now and then, however, you may have to fire a client if you can't work with her successfully.

Yep, I said, "Fire your clients."

I'm surprised at how many entrepreneurs still feel like they can't fire clients. The fear of not getting anyone to replace a bad apple keeps them paralyzed in a cycle of resentment and overwork, but that negative client who calls you nonstop and is still never satisfied is not helping you grow your business. She is not recommending you to friends, supporting the expansion of your business, or contributing to your team in any meaningful way. Money alone is not enough reason to sacrifice your peace of mind, morale, or standards.

That negative client who calls you nonstop and is still never satisfied is not helping you grow your business.

Worse, this client may even be sabotaging your relationship with other clients by badmouthing you or trying to get others to join her negative bandwagon. By firing the ringleader of this client circus, you will usually tame the rest of them. I don't mean that you get off the hook for meeting their legitimate needs, but you will probably be able to salvage working relationships with most of those people if they aren't being spurred on by one negative person.

The key to firing a client is to clearly state your expectations from the start. Distribute your rules or guidelines to all customers. Then when someone isn't following those rules, you have every right to tell her "this isn't a good fit" due to that particular guideline.

I recommend a warning first. I might say something like, "I've noticed you've had several complaints about the way we run our business and that you disagree with a lot of our policies and procedures. I'm not sure our business is the right fit for you." Very quickly, you will see this person either coming around to your way of thinking or becoming even more volatile.

One word of caution: No matter how you feel about an outgoing client, do your best to end the relationship on a positive note. Tell her you're sorry things didn't work out, and wish her the best of luck.

I can tell you that my company's atmosphere has greatly improved since I started firing clients who weren't a good fit for how we do business. By letting them go, I made room for new, appreciative clients who have helped us grow even further.

BUILD STRATEGIC PARTNERSHIPS

The people you do business with are just as important as your customers are. How you treat vendors and other businesses in your community will come back to you in ways you can't even imagine. The trouble with these relationships is that most entrepreneurs look at what they can get from these people. It's not about what you can get from them. It's about giving them value first.

In the Business Rescue Roadmap, we'll look at the relationships in light of how positive, negative, or neutral they are right now when it comes to influencing your success. But for now, give some thought to who is in your business life and what opportunities you might be missing out on.

When working with large vendors, I always try to get my own representative. I like speaking to the same person every time, building that relationship, and knowing I can count on that person if I'm ever in a bind. My reps know that I'm loyal, honest, and timely in my payments, so they often go out of their way to help me. This wouldn't be possible if I hadn't taken the time to build relationships with each of them and give them the kind of respect and attention they need to do their own jobs.

Treating your vendors well also promotes your prospect list. When vendors are treated well, they know that you also treat your customers well, and they're happy to recommend you.

I work hard to build relationships with other businesses in my community. It's important to have connections to many different people—not just those in your industry—because referrals come from all sides.

To make these connections, I regularly reach out to other businesses I admire. I tell them I love the work they do or that I had a great experience with their business. Then I tell them if they ever need help promoting anything to let me know. Often, I promote another business's event in our newsletter or at the school with a poster. After we've promoted for them, they are usually quick to help promote our events as well.

Next time you have a promotion coming up, plan a few months in advance. Rather than canvasing the area with your fliers or asking strangers to help you with promotions, first see how you can help other businesses. After a month or two of helping others, the business owners who were once strangers will feel like community partners. They'll *want* to help you promote your event. Isn't that a much better relationship?

Also, keep in mind that appreciation gifts aren't just for clients. For some of our key partners, we keep a calendar of promotions. Once a month, we select a vendor and send a small gift to them. This might be chocolate-covered strawberries or a gift basket. For example, Jimmy John's donated sub sandwiches for an event of ours. Afterward, I ordered a jumbo frosted cookie cake that read, "Thank You Jimmy John's!" and personally walked it into their store. It probably cost me about $10 and took me twenty minutes to run it over there, but the manager was so grateful and happy. And now I've built a relationship—not just with a business, but with a person.

Business owners are people, so treat them well. Remember what they care about and what's important to them, and find ways you can help.

Another great way to build relationships is by donating to a common cause.

We regularly host events. We foot the bill, put on the event, and do all the advertising. All the work is on us. We ask other businesses if they'd like to sponsor a portion of the event—the food or the balloons, for example. We put their logo on a postcard we're sending out to thousands of people. Not only is that free advertising for them, it's also increased credibility for us. If the event benefits a local or national charity, the donation amount rises significantly when we involve others. Then, we and our sponsors get the satisfaction of a big donation as well as increased involvement from the community.

In one case, our hosting a charity event resulted in a local hair salon's reaching out to us and asking us to be a sponsor of their hair fashion show. For a small fee, we were able to get a promotional packet into everyone's goody bags.

The same scenario can play out for an online event. For example, if you're hosting a webinar, part of your proceeds can benefit the cause of your choice. You can enlist other businesses to sponsor a portion of the webinar cost in exchange for advertising, and then you as a group are raising money and providing a valuable educational webinar.

I've found that these partnerships are strategic to my business growth—and they are personally enjoyable as well. I make friends with other business owners, but long before that, we establish a professional respect. These community partners are going to think of us immediately when asked about a good dance school in town. They're also often willing to help spread the word about our events or promotions without anything in return because they know they're promoting a respectable business.

I can't tell you how many times that a sponsor who has donated something to the event comes up to me afterward and thanks me for the opportunity to advertise to my clients. Sponsors usually tell me they can't wait to do something for me in return. Good position to be in, right?

TRAIN A WINNING TEAM

None of what I do would be possible without the incredible staff that works so hard every day to ensure our school is a success and our students are happy. I didn't always have this kind of team support.

After attending my first professional seminar, the summer after my first year in business, I was flooded with ideas. You know how it is. You go to a seminar, and you get so many ideas you can't keep up. The trouble is that there is no way you're going to implement all of those ideas—and continue to run a business—all on your own.

I knew I had to get people to help me put all of those new ideas into place. As I left that conference room and dreamed of returning the next year as a bigger player, I renewed my commitment to make my school better than ever. To do that, I had to make some major changes in our day-to-day operations.

When I got home, I put out an ad on Craigslist and spread the word locally. By September, I had hired several new team members. Not all of them are still with us, but a few are. I found some real gems.

Hiring

How did I find the right people? Even though I was urgently ready to hire, I didn't hire out of desperation. I followed some guidelines to make sure I hired the best people for the jobs I had available.

First, I looked for someone who was friendly and nice. I can train someone to answer the phone correctly, teach her about the various types of dance, and coach her on customer service . . . but I can't train someone to be a good person. I can't train her to be outgoing and smile at strangers. This stuff is inherent in who we are, so I looked for people who exuded friendliness in their interviews.

Second, I looked for someone who presented herself well from day one. That means that how she showed up for the interview needed to be good enough that I would put her out there with my clients right then if necessary. If she wasn't dressed properly, behaving politely, or responding clearly in an interview, she would be highly unlikely to do those things once hired. In fact, I've noticed that behavior like that usually goes downhill from there.

One of the surprising keys to hiring the right person is discovering someone who knows her value.

Third, I didn't settle. I knew what skills, personality, and presentation I needed. Period. No exceptions. I knew that this meant I might be waiting months to find the right fit, but I was willing to wait—and I was willing to pay enough for the right person. Hiring someone who wasn't quite right for our culture or our clients would only hurt us, and I had big dreams that didn't include cleaning up after a bad hire.

One of the surprising keys to hiring the right person is discovering someone who knows her value. Say I'm hiring a receptionist. Let's say that this position generally pays about $12 per hour. When a candidate comes in for an interview and says she'll take minimum wage, do I jump at the chance to save money?

No. I want the candidate who asks for $14 per hour. She has the industry experience to know the going rate, and she has the confidence in her skills to ask for what she thinks she's worth. That's someone I want on my team.

Training

When my new staff was in place, I was excited. And intimidated. It's one thing to run through the hiring gauntlet. It's another thing to train someone in your processes, procedures, and perspectives.

I've found that creating easily transferable checklists makes the onboarding and training process much simpler and more effective. When a new hire asks how to do something, I can usually answer, "There's a system for that!" We have written down what steps need to be taken and in what order we take them. We've noted what forms need to be filled out, who receives them, and when we do them.

The great thing about this checklist approach is that I can hand it off to any of my other leaders, and I know my onboarding and training will be carried out exactly as I like it to be.

> Creating easily transferable checklists makes the onboarding and training process much simpler and more effective.

Duties

The first person I hired was doing everything—teaching, answering phones, and taking payments. She was basically a mini version of me. I had been wearing multiple hats, and in the beginning, I could only afford to hire one other person to do the same.

When I hired a couple more people, though, the same thing happened. Each person was doing a little bit of everything. I needed to separate the duties into specific job descriptions. I started by figuring out what each person was good at and what she enjoyed doing. Then I put her in charge of something that made the most of her skills.

Sometimes when you've been in business for a while, you start to lose team members. Good ones. It's frustrating. I've discovered that being underused is often at the root of an employee's dissatisfaction. If people don't feel they're growing and being challenged, they will become bored and even negative. It's a short walk from negativity to a two-week's notice.

One employee really excelled at working with our community partners when she was given duties that fell in that area. She had a job title that was administrative, but over time, I realized I wasn't fully using her skill set—and she wasn't as satisfied as she might have been with a new opportunity for growth. So we created the role of community outreach coordinator. All of the little jobs that had fallen to various employees now came under one umbrella, and her old duties were distributed to others. Now, she's happy, we're happy, and our community partners are happy.

Morale

Team-building and morale don't come only from warm and fuzzy moments or quarterly events. Structure is a vital component in maintaining a healthy morale. Everyone in my company has a manager. My general manager reports to me. The other managers report to her. Then the teachers and administrative staff report to their respective managers. By allowing a leader in the company to support a small team, we give that leader the ability to reward and appreciate her team members.

Each quarter, every manager has a specific amount of money budgeted for employee gifts. When we hire someone, she fills out a "get to know you" form that lists her favorite things, such as chocolate, coffee, and movies. Throughout the year, her manager might buy her favorite coffee drink or give her a movie gift card. These unexpected little perks really keep up morale and help our staff feel appreciated.

We also give our employees birthday and Christmas gifts. These don't have to be pricey items, but acknowledging these events in people's lives further builds the personal connections and relationships all successful businesses are founded upon.

Each manager has a regular, one-on-one meeting with her team members. We always structure the meetings around three questions that are meant to maximize performance and improve morale.

1. Where did you win this week? This can be anything great that happened or that the employee accomplished. It reminds both the employee and the manager of this person's value and starts the meeting off on a positive note.

2. Where was there room for growth this week? The manager may already have an idea for this answer, but if the employee is the one who suggests it, the conversation goes much more smoothly. The atmosphere is more coaching than defensiveness because the manager isn't bringing up a mistake or rehashing a blunder that's already been discussed. Instead, the goal is to debrief, take an objective look at the issue, and come up with a better plan for next time.

3. Do you have any great ideas to make us the best in our industry? Discuss this topic last so the meeting also ends

on a positive note. Employees respond well to this because we regularly implement their ideas. When they see their work in action and experience how it adds value to the company as a whole, their morale skyrockets.

In addition to offering a fair salary for employees in their field, I also give merit raises every year, and I provide training and continuing education opportunities for my staff. In fact, I budget for this so I'm sure to present them with the chance to grow and achieve their own professional goals. Let me give you an example.

You'll be surprised at how many of your staff members aspire to be in leadership positions.

One day, our fantastically talented receptionist, Cara, told me she was going to quit. She was happy with her job, but her husband was in the military and was about to be deployed. She would have to stay home with her children while he was gone. Because she was such a stellar employee, my general manager and I brainstormed ways that she could work from home while her husband was gone. It was a big decision because we knew we'd still have the expense of hiring another receptionist to work at the school, but we felt the temporary expense was really worth keeping such a valuable member of our team. In the end, the work-from-home scenario worked out well for everyone, and Cara is still with us today. In fact, while brainstorming work we could give to Cara at home, I learned even more about delegating and was able to focus on bigger projects—like this book.

We also build company morale by offering optional meeting attendance to vision and planning sessions. You'll be surprised at how many of your staff members aspire to be in leadership positions. By allowing them to attend your strategic vision meetings—complete with lunch and a little socializing—you're helping them become more invested in the growth and success of your company. You're also showing them that you value their opinion and insights, while you help them see themselves as leaders.

Without someone to carry your vision into the next phase of your company's life, you will be chained to your desk forever.

Leadership

Developing leaders among your team is key to creating a business that can run itself without your constant intervention. Without someone to carry your vision into the next phase of your company's life, you will be chained to your desk forever.

I find it confusing when I meet entrepreneurs who are threatened by the thought of developing leaders on their own team. People who take initiative, who have bolder or better ideas than I do, and who are willing to work hard are the lifeblood of my business. I want to be surrounded by people who are smarter than I am—in at least some area—so we try to develop leadership among our staff at all levels of employment.

Remember that the people who work for you really work *with* you.

The most important thing is to lead by example. No one should be working harder on your business than you are. No one should be more excited about the future of your business than you are. And no one should be more understanding and supportive of your clients and your staff than you are. Keeping a positive attitude, maintaining regular hours, and refraining from gossip or complaining ensures that your team will follow suit.

No job is too small, and no task is too menial. I make sure that my staff sees me performing all sorts of duties in front of them so they know that nothing is off limits. I'm not better than anyone else is; I'm a team player, too. Modeling this attitude ensures that, as leaders rise up in your company, they will have the same can-do attitude.

Leadership is developed over time. If you recognize leadership potential in a staff member, tell her and ask about her vision for herself professionally. Even if she doesn't see herself with your company in years to come, helping her develop while she's with you will raise her morale and boost her performance.

Remember that the people who work for you really work *with* you.

The saying, "It takes a village to raise a child," could just as easily apply to your business baby. Among your team members, community partners, vendors, family and friends, mentors, and peers, you are surrounded by resources and support. Take advantage of these resources by building relationships wherever you go. See what you can give rather than what you can get. You'll be surprised at what comes back to you.

SIGN POSTS

You're in the business of building relationships. No matter what you do with your business, anyone you work with impacts your success, so make these relationships count.

1. Who has acted as your mentor in the past? A parent, teacher, or fellow entrepreneur? Perhaps an author who wrote an inspiring, foundational book on personal growth? I have always looked up to John Maxwell, for example. Reflect on who you might look to today for mentorship.

2. What system do you have in place for training your team how to treat clients? Are you leaving it all up to how team members feel on a particular day? Don't leave this vital aspect of training to chance.

3. The best way to develop relationships wherever you go is to see what you can give rather than what you can get. Make a list in your journal of people you'd like to form partnerships with, and brainstorm how you might give them something of value via your time or talents.

CHAPTER SEVEN

When you come to a crossroad in life or in business, you need a guide. How else will you know which path leads you in the direction of your goals?

After working with entrepreneurs who despaired of saving their businesses, I developed a system I call the Business Rescue Roadmap. This step-by-step process cuts through the clutter and confusion you feel and helps you pinpoint exactly what areas need urgent change—and which steps you can take to make those changes.

As you read this chapter, I'll ask you to make notes in a journal, so grab a notebook. It doesn't need to be anything fancy. This is your chance to ink it, not just think it. You'll be answering questions as well as downloading specifically tailored worksheets. I created all of these materials to coordinate with your specific goals and to highlight your areas of challenge. You'll also come away from each worksheet, quiz, and questionnaire with a clearer understanding of what you can do to improve your situation and how you can take yourself and your business to the next level.

I encourage you to walk through this section the first time with your top priority in mind. (We'll talk about this in the next section.) After you've done that, walk through it again with your next area of challenge. Then do it again . . . and again. I hope you'll use this chapter and the accompanying materials throughout the next several months and even years of your business life.

The intent of the Business Rescue Roadmap isn't only to point out where you're going astray. It's also to empower you to get back on the right path toward success . . . and stay there.

Are you ready to get started? Take out your journal and let's do it!

THE REALITY CHECK

Step One: Are you in the right business?

Without passion, purpose, and meaning, no entrepreneur will be satisfied with even the most successful business. Let's evaluate where you stand in this fundamental passion before we look at any specific areas of your business.

Answer these questions honestly. You're not out to impress anyone here. You don't need to prove anything. If you're not honest, and if you continue down a path that's not right for you, others will suffer with you. Read each question, and get real with yourself.

1. Do I feel in my heart of hearts that I'm supposed to be an entrepreneur?

2. Am I willing to take the risks, criticism, and responsibility that go with owning a business?

3. Does my business allow me to pursue my passion?

4. Do I find purpose and meaning in my work with my business?

5. Do I have a dream for the future of my business?

If you answered "Yes" to all five questions, then move to the next step.

If you answered "No" to any of these questions, this is a red flag. Pay attention to this warning. It doesn't necessarily mean you need to abandon your business altogether, but it probably means you need to make some major changes if you're going to save it.

Look back at the question you answered "No" to, and take a few minutes to write in your journal about why you feel this way.

Remember that you may have a great business idea, but if you're not willing to do what's necessary to be an entrepreneur, you may need help. Perhaps it's time to find someone else to help run the business so you can step away. Or maybe you need to instill more of your passion into your business, shift gears to a different product or service, or focus more on community efforts and giving back. If you find yourself without a vision for the future, take time now to brainstorm. Sometimes a lack of vision can mean that it's time to walk away, and sometimes it means you haven't had time to create those big dreams. This is the perfect opportunity to take some time and get yourself excited again.

I suggest you call a trusted advisor to help you brainstorm your next step. Don't panic. Just talk it out, and take one thing at a time. Be real with yourself. Stepping away from your business doesn't mean you're a failure. It means you're successful enough as a business owner to understand when to cut your losses.

Step Two: Look at the problem.

The first time I was faced with the question, "Is my business worth saving?" I had a million questions. What could I afford? Were my skills a match for what needed to be done? Could I hire help . . . and how much?

It's time to dump all the questions spinning around in your head. Use this space—and another piece of paper if needed—to write down every question you have about the state of your business. Address financial concerns, staffing fears, marketing issues, and personal problems in detail. Don't skip anything because it's minor, silly, or irrational. Write down every question and concern you have. Your journal is your safe place.

Now that you have all that junk from your head out onto paper, you should be able to think a little more clearly about where to start.

Go back through your list and pick out the Top Three Issues that are holding you back. What three things will keep your business from succeeding if you don't answer or solve them soon? Is it a lack of effective marketing to reach the right clients? Is it a lack of sleep, self-discipline, or personal well-being that's pushing you into burnout? Does financial debt threaten to eat all of your future profits? Do you lack an effective team to back up your efforts on the front lines? Are you so overwhelmed with to-do lists that you can't see straight? Pick your Top Three Issues, and write them in your journal like this:

Top Three Issues

1.

2.

3.

Now, of those three, select one Master Goal that you will focus on as we move through the rest of this chapter and develop your Business Rescue Roadmap. You can come back through this chapter and work on the other two later, but for now, focus on the first one only so you can be thorough and take effective action right away.

Keep in mind that you're never going to be completely finished with the first category. Change is a long process, but at some point, you'll start seeing positive results that will encourage and motivate you to start on your second category.

The fundamental idea I want you to get out of this process is this: changing even one thing can make a huge difference.

Feel free to skip sections that don't apply to your Master Goal. Come back to them later when you're ready to tackle the other two of your Top Three Issues.

YOUR REFLECTION IN THE MIRROR

Most female entrepreneurs are incredible people. They're strong, insightful, talented, and visionary. I love meeting other women in business because we tend to have similar personalities. Of course, we also have similar challenges.

It never ceases to amaze me how many entrepreneurs don't realize that their personal well-being and mental attitude affect their ability to succeed in business. I meet smart, capable women who aren't reaching their potential because of some very controllable issues.

Head over to my website at StacyTuschl.com/Tools and download the worksheet called "Self-Sabotage." With it, you'll create a clear map of where to begin the all-important work of personal growth.

Who you are defines the parameters of your business—good and bad. The more you work on yourself each day, the better chances your business has for success. Put down your journal and head to the Tools page. You don't want to miss this step.

MONEY MATTERS

Most entrepreneurs have some kind of struggle with money. Whether it's lack of security, towering debt, or simply budgeting inexperience, we all have a learning curve when we start a business.

Before you can decide how to take steps to remedy your money matters, you have to figure out where you stand. Visit StacyTuschl.com/Tools and take the "Money Matters" quiz. This extensive questionnaire will help you determine which financial challenges are holding you back and what you need to fix first.

SPREADING THE WORD

Some people say that the most essential element of a successful business isn't the product or service, the employees, or the location. It's the marketing. I couldn't agree more. If you don't get the message out about your business, no one will buy from you. Without clients, you don't have profit, and without profit . . . well, we all know where this is headed.

Your marketing is vital to the survival of your business.

One of the least-understood aspects of marketing is that it's emotional. People look at ads for all sorts of reasons: great prices, handsome models, bright colors, or big fonts. But people *buy* your product or service in large part because of how you make them feel. They feel good when they think of doing business with you.

In this section, we're going to take a look at how you feel about your brand and your marketing in general. Then we'll get specific about what strategies might help you take your efforts to the next level.

Go to StacyTuschl.com/Tools and download the worksheet called "Marketing to Emotions." By the time you've filled it out, you'll have some detailed strategies for moving forward.

THE SELF-SUFFICIENT BUSINESS

Can you imagine being able to take a month away from your business . . . without worrying about it functioning and continuing to be profitable while you're gone? Or owning a business that manages itself day to day so you can focus on the future? In my opinion, that's the goal.

Creating a business that runs itself, rather than running you, means true time and financial freedom. But how do we get there? If you're wearing all the hats and operating on a shoestring budget, that kind of self-sufficient business can seem a long way off. But no matter where you are in the life cycle of your business, there are things you can do to make that kind of company a reality.

Take out your journal, and let's get to work on what I think is one of the most essential of entrepreneurial skills.

Delegation

To take control back from the business, you have to let go. Entrepreneurs generally have a tough time letting go of control when it comes to daily tasks, so I'm going to take you through a step-by-step delegation guide.

No matter how well you think you're already delegating, follow these steps, and I guarantee you will discover ways that you can take more off your plate and get more done in the process. Remember the story about Cara, our receptionist, in chapter 6? Now that I have someone I can delegate to regularly, I'm able to do more because I have that person in place.

1. Make a list of every single task you dislike in your day.

2. Add to your list every task that isn't your strong suit; in other words, list the tasks that you're not trained or educated to do but that you do anyway.

3. Combine similar tasks into job descriptions for someone else. This is how you can delegate multiple tasks at once.

4. Now make a list of your regular tasks that you enjoy or are especially good at.

5. Add to that list of positives the tasks that you wish you could do if you only had the time.

6. Combine these tasks into your own job description. Your goal moving forward is to do only what's on this description.

7. Now, pull out your budget. (No budget? Visit the section in this chapter called "Money Matters.") Get tough and scrutinize your budget for an extra $100 or more per month.

8. Visit StacyTuschl.com/Tools and you'll discover a list of websites that will help you find a contract worker, full-time employee, or service provider (depending on what you can afford).

A word of caution: Don't wait on this. Too many times, I hear business owners say, "I know I need to delegate, but I just haven't done it yet." Putting off this vital step only hurts your company's potential and can even harm your well-being if you're doing too much. Take care of yourself and your business by bringing in some help. Even an hour a week is a start.

Scheduling

Taking control of your calendar will help you manage the tasks you really want to do, and it will create boundaries that protect your off-work time.

The first and most immediate action you can take in this area is to stop trying to accomplish every random thing on your to-do list in one day. Commit to three small goals each day. If they're aligned with your priorities, you'll really propel yourself forward with even the smallest consistent actions.

Next, I've developed a "One-Day-To-Do List" I'd like you to follow for overhauling your calendar system and a "Scheduling Your Priorities" method for determining whether your schedule matches your priorities. Download these from StacyTuschl.com/Tools.

THE BUSINESS OF PEOPLE

I started my business as a solopreneur. It was just me and seventeen clients (students, in my case). But as I've said, even back then, it took a village to run my business. The people in my life weren't all officially part of the business, but they each contributed in some way. The parents of my students helped me find the courage to charge my first fees. My own parents helped me with location. My grandparents inspired me to incorporate.

Evaluate who the major influences are in your business life. Download the worksheets titled "Influence," "Partnerships," and "Teamwork" at StacyTuschl.com/Tools. Complete them with one goal in mind: honesty. It can be hard to look objectively at the people in our lives, especially those we care about. But if you want your business to succeed, you have to be realistic about who is truly influencing it and how.

YOUR BUSINESS RESCUE ROADMAP

Now that you've completed the most pertinent sections and addressed the most urgent issues in your business success or failure, it's time to create a master plan.

Take out your journal and set a Master Goal. Maybe it's becoming financially solvent, having a dynamic, effective team, or creating a sparkling rebrand and marketing reboot.

From this master goal, work backward and create smaller goals that you can meet along the way. Use the worksheets and questionnaires from your Master Goal section to help you with these steps.

Then, for each of these smaller goals, create daily tasks, habits, and attitudes that will help you accomplish them.

Each day, work on at least one of these activities to move you toward your Master Goal.

FINAL WORD

As we close this final chapter, I want you to know something: You are worth saving. Yes, I know that this book is about your business and whether it's worth saving, but too many of us confuse our self-worth with our business or financial worth.

I know the truth about you. You are already a success. How do I know this? Because you picked up this book. You read and took notes, or you downloaded worksheets. You gave serious thought and took actions. You talked with others. You dreamed and brainstormed. You got real with yourself and took a hard look at the people in your life. You were willing to be uncomfortable.

Join me for the Focused Formula Bootcamp, and go beyond surviving to thriving. Sign up today at StacyTuschl.com.

You see, you're already ahead of your competition in so many ways because of your willingness to face facts and do something about them.

In fact, I'm so sure that you're the kind of person who will succeed in your business that I want to extend a special invitation to join me for my exclusive Focused Formula Bootcamp. I hope you'll take the next step in not only surviving but thriving as an entrepreneur by joining me at the live event or signing up for the online course. You'll gain keys to mastery in areas like focus, discipline, and productivity—keys that you won't find anywhere else. For a dedicated, courageous, and innovative entrepreneur like yourself, the Focused Formula Bootcamp could be the boost you need to achieve your biggest goals.

Whether your business is successful right this second or not, *you*, my friend, are successful. You are worth saving. You are worth time, effort, investment, and resources. Your dream has meaning. Your life has purpose. And if you take the time for professional and personal growth each day, I know, without a doubt, that your business will be just as successful as you already are.

So make me proud. Make yourself proud. Do one thing today that's different. Take one step in the direction of your dreams. Make today the day you begin to save your business!

ABOUT THE AUTHOR

Stacy Tuschl is an author, speaker, entrepreneur, and business coach. At the age of 18 in her parents' backyard, Stacy began what would become The Academy of Performing Arts. Today, the school serves thousands of clients in two custom-built Wisconsin locations, and Stacy is a sought-after coach for her experience-based counsel. As the creator of the online course, Focused Formula Bootcamp, Stacy shares proven strategies to help women entrepreneurs achieve balance by focusing and acting on their most important goals. Stacy's driving passions are her husband, Kent, and her two beautiful daughters, Tanner and Teagan.

FOCUSED FORMULA BOOTCAMP

Take back control of your business and your life with this mini-course from entrepreneur and business coach Stacy Tuschl. Stacy has never shared these tactical and time-saving video tips before now.

IN THESE VIDEOS, YOU'LL GET:

- Real-life tips for deleting distractions

- An amazing five-minute strategy for focusing your day

- A system to prioritize your goals

- The cure for the time-stealer known as your smartphone

- Stacy's personal productivity calendar method

- And more tools you need to regain your focus, energy, and time.

SIGN UP AT WWW.FOCUSEDFORMULABOOTCAMP.COM

**Congrats on making it to the end!
Here's your FREE GIFT to hit the ground
running for the next 30 days:**

With my free guide

10 Effective Ways to Get
More Dream Clients Quickly

This Guide reveals everything you need to know to build
your dream business filled with your <u>dream</u> <u>clients</u>.

We're talking about building a roster of <u>raving</u> <u>fans</u>
that experts charge thousands of dollars to tell you.

Here's What You'll Learn:

- 10 different ways to attract the right people and
  some you can implement immediately today

- Maximize your visibility & authority, and double
  your conversions

- How to gain new clients while you're sleeping

**Visit www.StacyTuschl.com/Dreamclients
to get your free guide**

Made in the USA
Coppell, TX
04 September 2024

36830371R00095